Heart Murmurs

What Patients Teach Their Doctors

For Linda —
Know you'll Keep
the heart in your
work.
Sharon

Perspectives in Medical Humanities

Perspectives in Medical Humanities publishes scholarship produced or reviewed under the auspices of the University of California Medical Humanities Consortium, a multi-campus collaborative of faculty, students and trainees in the humanities, medicine, and health sciences. Our series invites scholars from the humanities and health care professions to share narratives and analysis on health, healing, and the contexts of our beliefs and practices that impact biomedical inquiry.

General Editor

Brian Dolan, PhD, Professor of Social Medicine and Medical Humanities, University of California, San Francisco (UCSF)

Recent Titles

Clowns and Jokers Can Heal Us: Comedy and Medicine
By Albert Howard Carter III (Fall 2011)

Health Citizenship: Essays in Social Medicine and Biomedical Politics
By Dorothy Porter (Winter 2011)

What to Read on Love, Not Sex: Freud, Fiction, and the Articulation of Truth in Modern Psychological Science
By Edison Miyawaki, MD, Foreword by Harold Bloom (Fall 2012)

Patient Poets: Illness from Inside Out
Marilyn Chandler McEntyre (Fall 2012) (Pedagogy in Medical Humanities series)

Bioethics and Medical Issues in Literature
Mahala Yates Stripling (Fall 2013) (Pedagogy in Medical Humanities series)

www.UCMedicalHumanitiesPress.com

brian.dolan@ucsf.edu

This series is made possible by the generous support of the Dean of the School of Medicine at UCSF, the Center for Humanities and Health Sciences at UCSF, and a Multi-Campus Research Program (MRPI) grant from the University of California Office of the President.

Dedicated to my sons Matthew and Nicholas

.

Heart Murmurs

What Patients Teach Their Doctors

Edited by Sharon Dobie, MD

First published in 2014

by UC Medical Humanities Press

UCMedicalHumanitiesPress.com

Cover Art by Eduardo de Ugarte

Designed by Virtuoso Press

Author photo Theresa Halzle photosbyt.com

Library of Congress Control Number: 2014948700

ISBN: 978-0-9889865-5-8

Printed in USA

Contents

Chapter 8   Bias, Assumption, and Learning Tolerance   137

Chapter 9   Can I Really Know You? … Or Anyone?   151

Chapter 10   My Patient as a Mirror   163

Chapter 11   Self-Acceptance   183

Epilogue: Our stories and the ethics of writing about patients   209
Authors' Biographical Notes   212

Acknowledgements

Sharon Dobie

Manuscripts become books and writers become authors with a community supporting them. Though writing may be solitary, at least for extroverts, there is a lot of chewing, advice seeking, and hand wringing about the work, out loud and in the world. All of us who publish share credit with supporters, editors, contributors, and whoever allowed us (or at least did not prevent us from having) the space to think about something and put those thoughts to paper. This book would not be here without so many individuals. I know that the authors represented here would have their own people to thank; hopefully some of mine reflect who theirs would be.

Back in 1973, I decided medicine would be a better career for me than social policy planning. UC Berkeley let me come back and do pre-med work and the University of California in San Francisco (UCSF) educated me to be a physician. Their Family Medicine program at San Francisco General Hospital (SFGH) trained me in the science and art of our work, with an avant-garde methodology. I spent my intern year being watched in clinic through a one way mirror by a behavioral science provider and a family medicine doctor. I was often called out of the exam room not to discuss what I thought was the main issue (the ear ache, the fever, the well child exam), but to explore the subtext in the family narrative. I was as cantankerous and out spoken then as I am now. One of my key faculty mentors, Ron Goldschmidt MD, wrote in a graduation gift something to the effect that he enjoyed (translate: probably sometimes found me frustrating and other times humorous) "growing with me." Thank you UC Berkeley, UCSF, and Family Medicine at SFGH for my education and training; you were instrumental in shaping how I live my life as a physician.

To all of our patients: thank you. You teach us daily. This book is just a sampling. And you give us so much more with your trust, your concerns for us, and the friendships you allow. To those of you who are specifically represented here and who have read and allowed the publication of our shared time, we are forever grateful.

We thank the University of California Medical Humanities Press for publishing this work and hope that readers will think of supporting this non-profit whose mission is dedicated to publishing books in the medical humanities and whose ability to do so is dependent on grants, contributions, and royalties from what they publish.

Some specific thanks go to some key people. Valerie Ross is the University of Washington Family Medicine Residency Behavioral Science faculty lead. She listened to my musings about Relationship Centered Care and discussed and offered suggestions for a piece I was writing for *Academic Medicine.* From that we created the workshop we have been doing since that time for our third year residents, at national workshops with seasoned physicians, in other residencies, and for faculty at two medical schools. Most of the authors represented here wrote their pieces in one of these workshops. I appreciate Valerie's stalwart support for this project and her foreword. I think more than 500 physicians have completed our workshop; every story has moved us. I thank all who participated, even when challenging, and for their honesty and self-reflection. What has been and is striking to both Valerie and me is that we doctors struggle with actually stating how much and actually naming what we have been given within this work we do. The courage of the authors represented here may seem trivial; it is not. To come forward and share what is learned in tough situations requires an ability to be vulnerable. For that reason, all those who allowed me to work with them and their stories are included; there was no selection process except for one story which was excluded because of the vulnerability of the patient about whom this physician wrote. Thank you all.

Early on and throughout the development of this book, there were two others who were key. They met with me often, encouraged me to not drop the project, read early stories and organizational schemas, commented, prodded, read more, and joined me over many dinners where this book was a topic of conversation. Thank you to Barbara Matthews and Denise Lishner who both worked in the research section of the University of Washington Family Medicine Department and who both beat me to retirement. Thank you also to my sister Donna Bonds and colleague Rachel Lazzar who, along with Valerie, Barbara, and Denise, read an early "complete" manuscript. All of their comments were invaluable in the multiple revisions that followed.

Thanks to my department for granting me a partial sabbatical that allowed me the space to conceptualize how to bring these stories together into a cohesive work. Thank you to Judith Lightfoot, who generously provided insightful and very useful editing suggestions, to my dear friend Joan Lamphier who did a last proof read, and to Theresa Halzle for donating my picture on the cover.

To Hedgebrook and the writers who were there when I was granted a three week residency in 2012: Thank you. Hedgebrook, on Whidbey Island in Washington state, is another non-profit deserving of support in their work to support "women writers authoring change." The staff nurtured us and met our every need with incredible meals and great company. Tucked away in the woods, the six cottages that house the six writers in residence provide about as idyllic an environment as one can imagine. Those three weeks were a quiet time to write and edit, mixed with social time in the evenings with gifted writers whose feedback moved this manuscript forward from social message to hopefully approaching literary value.

As I neared submission, I revisited the ethics of how we approach writing about patients. Actually, I had both a panic attack and a breakdown. Luckily, I only spent about twelve hours convinced we could not publish the work. Then I contacted two people and I will be forever grateful for Doctors Kelley Edwards (faculty in Bioethics and Humanities at the University of Washington) and Johanna Shapiro (Director, Program in Medical Humanities & Arts, Family Medicine, University of California, Irvine) for their quick response and willingness to talk. Conversations with them reinforced what I know: these are muddy waters and I have been thoughtful and careful.

Last and most importantly, thank you to my kids, friends, and co-workers who each and all offered encouragement, suggestions, title ideas, and who put up with my hand wringing these past few years.

Foreword

Valerie Ross MS
Director, Behavioral Science Education
University of Washington Family Medicine Residency

I love listening to people's stories, and helping them become aware of the stories they are living, and to live the stories they prefer. That's my job. I am a psychotherapist. I also teach physicians-in-training about communication and healing in medicine.

Sharon had been working on a journal submission on Relationship Centered Care, mindfulness, and self-awareness and we met several times to discuss the concepts that were the material for this paper.[1] Then one day we sat down together at lunch and drew up a workshop idea. We wanted to help physicians tell stories about how they come to know themselves better within and through relationships with their patients. We called it the "Gifts Workshop." I was thrilled; this workshop brought together my work as a psychotherapist and as a teacher of physicians.

We had no idea what fruit that first workshop would bear. There we were, giving a short presentation on Relationship Centered Care, mindfulness, and narrative, followed by a writing prompt. We were excited, curious, and a little nervous. That small group of physicians dove in. It was quiet while they wrote. When it came time for volunteers to read their pieces, each participant glanced around the room, deciding if they felt ready. When they did read, each usually took a deep breath before starting, a silent acknowledgement of the vulnerability it takes to share these stories out loud. For physicians who have the courage to read their stories out loud in these workshops, young or seasoned, there is always a moment of discovery. It is usually an emotional moment where some insight, or a tender spot, is

---

1   Dobie S. Reflections on a well- traveled path; self-awareness, mindful practice, and relationship-centered care as foundations for medical education. *Academic Medicine* 2007; 82(4):422-27.

revealed. The "gifts" this first group reflected were wide ranging. Theirs were stories about loosing and finding compassion, striving for and giving up on perfection, and accepting what is beyond one's control. All the stories expressed strong emotions: joy, sadness, anger, fear, guilt.

Sharing the story invites intimacy among the workshop participants. There is vulnerability both in the telling and in the listening where one opens up to being touched, changed or to recognizing oneself in the other's story. Arthur Frank, a medical sociologist whose work Sharon and I have drawn on, writes that reciprocity lies in the nature of story telling itself.[2] The reciprocity of story telling and listening echoes in these workshops from patient to physician, and then to other physicians. We continued to offer these workshops in our own institution and around the country. Many of the stories in this collection were first written down and spoken out-loud in these settings.

The idea for the book emerged out of this experience. We asked ourselves: Who was listening to, or speaking about, the life lessons physicians learned in relationship with their patients? We came to believe that it was important to acknowledge the reciprocity involved in the healing relationships: for the physicians so these invisible stories could be seen, heard and felt, and for patients so they could know that even in their hardest times, they are powerful teachers. And are we not all patients at some point?

Nourished by these stories of reciprocity between doctor and patient and as a therapist, this listening helps me to think more about how the patients I see enrich my own life. As a teacher of physicians it helps me to know more about the struggle of learning to be a healer in a culture that does not support making time to pay attention to the depth of the relationship that is occurring every day between doctors and patients. And listening to these stories helps me to respect the deep caring and commitment that physicians hold for those they serve at birth, death, and in the many many, moments in between.

I hope readers of this collection will be fed and touched by these stories because these narratives ultimately speak to what is true in all relationships. Perhaps they may strike a cord somewhere in your heart and encourage you to think about reciprocity in your own relationships. Maybe you will be

---

2   Frank AW. *The Wounded Storyteller: Body, Illness, and Ethics.* University of Chicago Press, Chicago. 1995 (pg. 17-18).

moved to share those stories too. Finally, these stories are testimony to this: there is medicine in relationships. Sometimes we need to take the time to reflect on these relationships to find the medicine, but it is there.

Introduction

Sharon Dobie

Over time, we learned that our role was contained in a single word: comfort. After a few days of visiting Harriet in her hospital bed and finding her slumped over the emesis basin, kerchief on her head, silent, and eyes downcast, she would be sitting up in bed with a little smile and open eyes, seeing us for the first time from that place of receding nausea. The only variable in the preceding days was her husband, Edwin. Was he sitting there as well, or not? He came from home every morning and sat by his silent, kerchiefed wife, patting her hand or reading his Bible; he returned home to sleep each night. We could keep her hydrated, and give a few medications that could help, but those helped only slightly.

Harriet was an elderly woman with diabetes and many complications. The most bothersome was her gastroparesis, a condition that reduces the ability of the stomach to empty its contents in an appropriate amount of time. At her best, she felt full all the time. In the middle of an attack, she had severe nausea, no appetite, and she vomited every time she tried to eat or drink even small amounts. These attacks brought her to the hospital almost every month.

In the early days, we became teammates between bouts, searching for a way to activate her stomach so that it would not fail her so painfully. We adjusted her medication and tried some wild ideas. There was the marijuana experiment that had her very proper African American community elder husband ready to drive across town to a Green Cross supplier to purchase supplies for us to cook up and suspend in a suppository, hoping it might get absorbed—she would have vomited anything taken by mouth. We never were able to try that experiment, but it was typical of how desperately we wanted to give her more days to face food and enjoy her life.

Our resident physicians worried about the frequency of her hospitalizations because nothing we did seemed to prevent a recurrence and inevitably, we would admit her again. Each time, the residents felt the anxiety of not being able to do more, yet eventually every time, the day would come when her smile would return. Slowly, after many admissions, they learned that fixing her was not the goal. Our job was to cradle her with our presence while she weathered the nausea and vomiting, her life contracted down to little communication with the outside world of family or even with her own medical providers. There was the bed, the emesis basin, few words, and sleeping when she could. When she was feeling better, she talked about her life at home, her garden, her husband, and the arguments among her adult children, her faith. And then she would go home until the next time. Gradually, our residents realized her admissions were not to be dreaded because we could do so little; they could be accepted for the graceful rhythm provided by patience—everyone's.

Over the ten years that her illness progressed and her kidneys failed, she and I often mused about why she still lived. We shared candid talks about who she was and her purpose on this earth. She said she had unfinished business in her family and she did not want to leave her husband. I suggested that she also was teaching our residents to be patient, to set aside the mindset that there is a "quick fix" for life's problems. With her elderly husband sitting at her side, stroking her hand for hours of each day, even that relationship of forty years modeled acceptance and a certain peace. During these conversations I spoke about how she was a participant in the relationships with her medical team, giving as well as receiving. The thought was not new to me; speaking it to her was. Harriet's surprise and pleasure at the notion of herself as a teacher and her grace in accepting her role were catalysts for the stories you will read in this book.

A visit to the "doctor"[1] is a narrative process, with patients' stories bringing them and their health care providers together. As the patient's story is told, heard, discussed, acted upon, reframed or molded, a relationship forms. I remember as a medical student wondering how people could just sit down and tell me about their lives, their dreams, their fears, their ills, long before I had anything to offer in answering their questions or treating them. I felt awkward, and yet it was my assignment: "Take the medical history, do

---

1   Doctor is in quotes because the health care team is not just physicians and includes physician assistants, nurse practitioners, nurses, pharmacists, therapists, and others. Many if not most people refer to their visits for health care as "going to the doctor." The stories and lessons in this book could be written and experienced by all of us who care for patients.

the physical exam, listen, and understand." The privilege of people trusting me with their story, trusting me to try to help them, took my breath away and when I left the room, I knew that trust was a gift. In the early days, I saw the gift mostly relating to how I would doctor; with each encounter, I learned more about a specific illness or condition, or maybe how to talk with a particular person. As my knowledge developed, I hoped some future patient might benefit from my learning. Over time, I started to see that these relationships and the stories that connected us also influenced my understanding of myself, of my relationships, and of my worldview. They contributed to what is whole in me, but I did not dwell on this awareness. After all, we were taught to give and serve, and it is almost heretical for a physician to acknowledge that our duty includes the receipt of something besides financial compensation. This shaping of my life by my relationships with patients remained a quiet presence for years.

Much attention is paid to the importance of the doctor-patient relationship for patients, but little is understood about how that relationship affects and changes the provider. How many of us as patients know the impact we have on those who care for us? Do we health care providers allow ourselves to reflect about the effect this work has on us? If we do reflect, do we only think of how we have taken the lessons offered by our work and carried them forward into our professional practice? How many of us are willing to explore these relationships and acknowledge their influence within our personal lives? I suspect many of us do not adequately give credit to these rich and meaningful experiences nor do we link the learning to our inner lives.

This book contains narratives written by physicians who agreed to write about their relationships with their patients and about what they received from those relationships. It seeks to illuminate ways that awareness and sometimes healing happen in the provider's heart. This is not a book for just doctors. Within these stories, I hope that all of us, for we all are patients at some time, see and recognize ourselves and appreciate our value. Into every relationship, we bring something of ourselves – even as a patient – that can and does impact the other person in ways we should not underestimate. I do also hope this book will encourage physicians and all health care providers to reflect on their relationships with their patients and to know themselves more deeply. In honoring these relationships, especially in a health care system that often leaves both providers and patients frustrated and disconnected, I hope they will find themselves invigorated in this very human work we do.

Physicians submitted the stories in this book as participants in workshops and as a few invited authors. Each contributor responded to this prompt: "Think of a particular relationship with a patient (be it a single encounter or an enduring tie) and tell what you learned from it about yourself. How is the gift you received from this person and this relationship manifested in your personal life?" In the workshop, after the writing exercise, small groups met and individuals read what they had written; the rest of the group commented on what they heard.

While you read the stories in this book, picture a group of 6-10 physicians sitting in a circle. They are varying ages, from all over the country, or they are a group of resident physicians in their last year of training. Someone volunteers to read aloud. The story of the patient flows easily (we are good at telling our version of patients' stories), intertwined with descriptions of the conversations, interventions, or feelings of the person reading the story. Imagine you see the face and eyes of the writer as the mood shifts, as voices get quieter, or maybe more agitated. There is no single emotion, but there is emotion. For a group rarely at a loss for words, actually naming or describing the lesson is sometimes challenging, sometimes initially skirted. Voices often choke, rise, or fall and invariably, writers acknowledge something of personal value in the relationship they describe.

Represented here are the pieces by all authors who worked with me on editing their work. I grouped their stories and my own by the themes they addressed. Each chapter opens and closes with a story by me and other stories of mine are scattered throughout the chapters.

For the reader to grasp the impact of the relationship on the physician, telling the physician's experience of the patient's narrative is important. Yet we knew we needed to present a respectful and careful view of the people about whom we wrote. To protect privacy of our patients, names, circumstances (age, gender, location, other circumstances), or both have been changed. Where the author's name is attached, permission was obtained from the patient or a family member, or if finding the person was not possible, the story is generic enough or has enough changed circumstances that the patients should feel protected. In some cases the interactions were very distant; obtaining permission was not possible. If the story was a respectful presentation and we believed recognition was unlikely, we allowed the story to be included. To further protect patients, for some stories the author is "anonymous." For two stories ("Amy Died" and "Grabbing Time"), family members gave permission to use the person's real name. One contributor died during the project and his family consented to publishing his narrative, although we could not locate his patient.

For each story I wrote, I obtained consent to publish it if the patient was still alive and could be found. For deceased patients, I obtained consent if I could reach a family member. I could not find some who were patients from decades ago or family members of some who had died. No current patient of mine should identify with any particular story as specific to her or him unless we discussed it.

For my patients: if you do not see yourself explicitly in these pages, please know that I probably spent hours planning to write about you and all that you taught and continue to teach me. Your lessons are reflected in this book. Thank you!

I believe that our patients' illnesses are metaphors for them and for us as well. There are days in my life where my appetite for living is blunted. I can be very much like Harriet: silent, gaze down, braced against the forces. My stresses win out temporarily, be they worries about my adult children, or work, or the pressures of the mundane. The fixer in me would like to barge in and repair or alter whatever is going on. Sometimes that choice works, but Harriet's cycles between nausea and a settled stomach remind me to slow down, to pause and remember the work of a person lying in a bed, nauseated, kerchief askance, modeling patience and acceptance, knowing that another day might remove the kerchief and return the smile.

You may recognize yourself in these pages, whether you are a patient or a provider. I hope the stories here will trigger memories and that your own stories surface. In the process of remembering, perhaps you too will see that the value of these relationships is larger than was apparent from the anecdote of the moment or the purpose of the medical encounter. If this book does anything to foster healing, it does so by drawing us all back to the basics: relationships matter.

Chapter 1

Connection

Invited In
Sharon Dobie

Steve, the dad, met me at the door just as a three year old half clad whirling dervish in a Superman cape jumped into the doorway and belted, "Dr. Dobie, where is Dr. Pelto?"

"He's on his way," I chuckled.

"Well, come here. I've got something to show you," he exclaimed as he bounded past his mother sitting on the couch, holding one baby, stopping at the porta-crib a few feet away. Jabbing his chubby finger between the slats of the crib he chortled. "Look, look! There's another one! There are two babies!"

"Wow!" and slapping my hand over my mouth, playing along, I added, "And who is whom?"

He easily identified each baby by his given name.

"Now come in here and see my games." And we were off, Superman and I, to the adjoining room as his mom laughed at his rapid-fire identification of his brothers by name. "He can tell them apart better than Steve and I can!"

Just a few days earlier, the atmosphere in the labor room had been almost festive. Jean and Steve arrived quickly when labor started. Carrying twins is hard work and they were happily looking forward to meeting their babies.

In 2012, the standard at our hospital was to deliver twins early. How early depended on the placenta(s). With twins like Jean's, having two placentas instead of one, we aimed for two weeks before the due date, or 38 weeks out of the usual 40 weeks. Preterm births are fairly common in twin or other multiple pregnancies, but Jean and the twins had made it to that 38-week mark. She was in labor! The day they arrived at Labor and Delivery, they had to decide if she would try labor and a vaginal birth of at least the first twin, or have a caesarian delivery right away. They chose to labor, setting a time a few hours hence as a decision point. If she were active and headed towards rapid delivery, they would proceed, hoping for a vaginal birth. If the dilation of her cervix was not significantly changed, they would proceed to a caesarian. Her only complication was that Twin B was not in an ideal position. Convention names the twin who is the first in line to deliver in a vaginal birth as Twin A, and Twin B is the one higher up in the uterus. Jean and Steve's babies settled into position with Twin A headed out headfirst and Twin B in the breech or seated position.

When the time came, there was no real change in her dilation and they chose to have their sons surgically delivered by the obstetricians on call that day. These two little downy blond babies were within ounces of each other in weight, and both had the perfectly shaped heads so common to babies born by caesarian section. Jean was walking the halls the day after surgery and every visit to their room found family and friends visiting and one of the babies nicely latched on her breast. The boys looked identical to me, but with two placentas, they might be identical twins and they might be fraternal. The family packed up and went home on the babies' third day of life, joining their three-year-old and Jean's mom, who had come to help.

We knew the newborn twins would need to be seen a few days after discharge from the hospital. All babies have risk of becoming jaundiced in the first days of life, with elevated bilirubin in the blood. Twins have a higher risk. Bilirubin is a breakdown product of red blood cells. It gets chemically changed in the liver and then passed into the intestine where it is excreted in the stool. A newborn's red blood cells turn over, dying and replaced by the bone marrow, more quickly than those of an older child's or an adult's. This puts more bilirubin into the blood stream. The newborn's liver is not always initially effective at converting the bilirubin and the level in the blood can rise. Other factors, including prematurity, bruising during birth, or incompatibility between maternal and fetal blood types, can also release more bilirubin into the blood stream in the early days after delivery. These babies did not have those other risks, but feeding and dehydration also play key roles and feeding twins is challenging to begin with.

For some, an elevated bilirubin is mild requiring nothing more than continuing to watch. Within a couple of days mom's milk comes in, and over days, the liver matures and more efficiently converts the bilirubin to a chemical that can be excreted. In those cases, it never reaches a level that requires "bili lights" in home or in a hospital readmission. If the serum bilirubin reaches a level that is considered dangerous for brain development, some babies do require "bili lights," the colored spectrum lights that chemically alter the bilirubin so it can be excreted, driving the level of bilirubin in the blood back to a safe level.

Knowing we would need to see and examine the twins and how hard it would be to bring the babies in to our clinic, Hank Pelto (one of our residents who had seen Jean along with me for prenatal visits and the delivery) and I offered to do a home visit. As we headed out to visit the family, we wondered if the twins would get enough nutrition and fluid in those first days to avoid the weight loss, dehydration, and jaundice that might put them under the "lights." We also thought Jean would benefit from our visit, because women who choose to breast feed twins deserve special support, not to mention that Jean was also recovering from her caesarian delivery.

Their home was a cozy older house on a quiet side street, a temporary rental big enough for their expanding family. The remodel of their house had fallen behind schedule and along with newborn twins, they were making do until they could really settle into their real home.

So there I was, being pulled into the energy and home of the Superman-caped big brother, his parents, his grandmother, and his baby brothers, who I could not tell apart. Once again my suggestion of an indelible pen tattoo of A or B on one foot of each was unanimously rejected.

The scene with big brother superhero was a replay when "Where is Dr. Pelto?" arrived, first identifying the babies, then pulling him to the adjoining room. Trains and cars and puzzles and books were strewn all over the floor, while a little boy wildly narrated the contents of the room, jumping from toy to toy, explaining his role or skills with each.

The twins were five days old when we made that home visit. The babies looked like newborns do, sleeping, feeding, gazing or crying, a pretty typical repertoire. Their older brother, the half-clad superhero, had the longest and fastest spoken run-on sentence in the household. In stark contrast, Jean would start to say something, and then, after a moment, as if she released the pause button, her words travelled slowly at about 85% of normal speed.

Steve was no different. Watching them and watching the three year old was like viewing a movie playing simultaneously at two speeds, with Hank and I adjusting and readjusting the speed of our speech, shifting back and forth between the two versions.

I was bemused but not concerned by these parents' visible fatigue—the incipient bags under their eyes and the slowed speed of their conversation. They had wisely taken to writing down who ate what when, who had a soiled diaper, or who slept, at least for the babies. We could see that one of the babies was jaundiced and would need the blood test for bilirubin level checked at the hospital. They set about organizing that outing.

"Who should go? Should we all go?"

"Should your mom stay here and we just take the one baby?"

"Do you want to go?"

"Do you?"

"Maybe we should all go and your mom stay here."

"Who should stay with her?"

"What about you and I go and just take Jacob?"

Hank and I offered support and suggestions, watching the scene unfold, around a three-year-old energy force batting balloons, building a tower, and thrusting his paper towards us to show how he wrote his letters.

While Steve packed diapers and other necessities, Jean's eyes looked like they would close at any moment. Then, looking around at the clutter of double car seats, double bags, pillows, the breast pump, strollers, her eyes rested on one of the babies. "This is a blast," she quietly laughed.

Did she mean it? Was she laughing because she could not keep track of anything nor easily organize the little trip for the lab test? Was the quiet in her voice just fatigue, or was it the crazy calm that sometimes comes with facing the unknown without unnecessary expectations? Almost incomprehensible was the calm into which we stepped—no, into which we were invited, as participants in that very moment of life.

When patients let us know they trust us with their care, or they invite us in to know them a bit better, or they ask about our families, or they notice we are tired, or many other gestures, we feel connected. Our job may be to focus on our patients and their needs, but whatever we call it, we are engaged in a conversation that takes place around a story that connects our patients and us. That may be one of the most important things we receive: connection.

Mick, Mack, and the Bars
Mick Storck

"Doctor, please call the VA Medical Center." It was the operator's familiar gravely voice—oddly a comfort zone in those years before cell phones and text pages. I answered and she patched the call through.

"This is Mack. (some labored breathing) I got a problem… Or at least I think it's a problem…(sighing) Am I going more nuts or what?" (sigh)So here it is…. There is this bar in my head … No, not that kind of bar. It's like a little gold bouillon cube. If I'm thinking something about the world, sometimes this bar turns blue… And sometimes it turns gray… And I think if the bar is blue then I can believe what I'm thinking.

If the bar turns gray then I think I shouldn't believe what I'm thinking. I've tried it out. I'm not sure if it works. What do you think?"

It was 9:30 p.m., a weekday evening, sometime in 1983; I was in the third year of my psychiatric residency. Mack, a semi-legend at our bustling Veteran's Hospital, had been diagnosed with paranoid schizophrenia only several weeks into his enlistment in the army. He was given a medical discharge and a "service-connected disability."

I first met Mack when he was admitted to our in-patient psychiatry service and I was a first year psychiatry resident only a couple of years older than him. After that admission, we met together at least monthly for two years. In my mind, I still see what I saw then: his long gangly arms and legs, marfanoid habitus, scruffy goatee, and in his longing eyes, his occasional sense of refuge when we met.

I can't remember exactly what I said to Mack. I'm the kind of person who tries like crazy to help people not feel so crazy or at least to not feel so alone with their late night worries and wonderings about their health, and that was true more than thirty years ago too. I probably said something like:

"Mack, what do you think? It's a cool thing you're calling me about; I'm glad you're talking this over with me and I don't think you necessarily need more Loxitane unless you're really afraid of bouillon cube bars in your head. … And, if I know you, Mack, you're probably at least a little intrigued with this idea! So keep track of this and let's see how it turns out. Call me tomorrow and we can talk more about this when we meet next week."

Something I know I thought then (but didn't say) and what I've thought about this "blue/gray bar" chat, at least every few weeks since then (and I wish I could be saying this to you right now, Mack) is:

"Mack there is barely a week that goes by when I don't hear your voice in my head, your sad, searching, hopeful, often lost – sometimes VERY lost, … but still connected and even at times playful voice. I hope (and, I suppose, believe) that somehow you have felt a bit safer in the world because of me. And you know what? I have felt a bit safer in the world, my world, our world, because of you! It still warms me up a little bit each time I think about it that you called me about your quandary." (Does that turn some bar in my head a warmer color on the spectrum?). We were both, then, less alone with our mid-evening musings.

I have told this story to many a student of the brain, student of health, student of medicine, residents, colleagues, and patients. It is a moment that speaks to how we relate, how we endure, how we belong to a kind of co-investigator kinship with our patients. We're all in this together. Did I help Mack to gain a bit more resilience in this world? I hope so, and if so, then maybe resilience, in part, is related to feeling a sense of shared flotation in the sea of life's vicissitudes and mysteries. The transactions of good medicine should do that. I know that patients often do better when they feel that the journey is shared, and I've learned that we "providers" do too. So who is "providing" for whom? I pass Mack's query on to you. Got any good bars in mind to share?

Learning to Connect
Kelly Glancey

Always searching for a connection with my patients, I found a great one the other week with Mr. Y, the kind of guy that made me love VA Hospitals. An old guy with lots of stories to tell, he started talking about his experiences in Pelileu and the islands in WWII. My grandfather had been stationed in the very same places, and this prompted me to call my grandmother that night to find out exactly where he had been and in what unit. It turned out they had been in the same regiment and battalion.

When I told him the next day, Mr. Y couldn't really remember that many names, but he thought they had probably met. My grandmother was so excited to hear this story that she sent me a newspaper review of a book that had photographs of the old tanks left behind in the South Pacific. I felt good that I could find this connection and at the same time, make my love of my career make sense to my grandmother. She was always hounding me about how neither my sister nor I were married or had kids.

I do see all these couples on labor and delivery having their first babies and I do want to have that for myself. My most memorable delivery this year was the twins. There was a lot of laughter in the room. Somehow the very funny dad was making the mom laugh despite her labor. The mom and dad just had this energy between them that permeated the room. She seemed so happy even though she was pushing out a baby – no, make that two babies. While I was working with them, the image of my boyfriend popped into my head. He is great at making me laugh and that's one of the reasons I love him. I could see us in the exact same spot as this couple, laughing, loving and having a baby. I wished he could be part of moments like this, where patients have trusted me to be part of a major event in their lives, and where that in turn lets me see a future similar scene that involves me or us.

My dad, also a doctor, once told me that this was his favorite part of medicine as well: the trust and entry into people's deepest moments. I do feel accomplished as a physician when someone opens up to me, but there is more. This also allows me to gain access to some of my deeper feelings.

It's kind of funny because I often feel success in my job, but often find myself wishing I could be more successful at my life. I was not particularly good with people when I was in high school, college and medical school. Part was shyness and part was just not being good at figuring out how to connect. Working with patients, there is an environment, a structure and purpose to interacting, where it is easier for me and it gave me practice and experience. Then too some of my patients' lives give me perspective. There are many other patient memories, like my first ever medicine patient who sang gospel to me. I realize that I have at least as much to learn from my patients as they from me and I am glad of that.

Postscript

I wrote the story above when I was a resident. Over time, I learned from practicing and can connect with people more closely in my personal life. It is still slow to come for me sometimes but I have gotten better. Now I am married to that funny boyfriend and we have twins. I know even more about connection, learning more with my husband and our relationships as a family.

The Last Dance

Sara Ehdaie

Rosie wheeled into my life with her daughter, Molly. At 92, Rosie was a slight woman, sitting in her wheelchair, hands quiet in her lap, and a calm smile on her relaxed face. Between her bouts of falling asleep in the office and her inability to tell me anything accurately about her day, Rosie's eyes would brighten and sparkle; she would tell a story punctuated with her hearty laughs.

Molly was a different matter. In that first visit, she informed me that she had just taken Rosie out of the nursing facility. Unsure about the care her mother had been receiving, she thought that she could take better care of her at home. Now she was uncertain if she had done the right thing. A long and frantic list of questions tumbled out, her voice rising, as she leaned forward, almost wringing the paper in her hand. She had questions about medications, about her mother's condition, and about her decision to bring her mother to live with her. With each additional question, it became clearer that she was at her wits' end, distraught, and overwhelmed. As I focused on trying to calm Molly, I understood that she was as much my patient as Rosie.

As we were talking, Rosie suddenly opened her eyes and they lit up as she told a tale about dancing with a handsome man the week before. She started humming the music, swaying her head in time with the melody, oblivious of her daughter's tumultuous emotions.

I looked at her daughter. "Molly?"

"It's true. They do have dances at the nursing home. I didn't realize how much Rosie would miss her friends and social activities," her daughter continued, "and she has been deteriorating since. She hardly eats and when she is not sleeping, she gets so confused and then has angry outbursts. I can't leave her alone for a minute. She's not calm like she is now, here. And she seems so sad."

We turned to Rosie one more time to let her finish her story. She told us again how happy she was when dancing a waltz. She hummed a tune and gestured with her arms and head, and I could picture her dancing.

There was more to handle than this one visit would allow and I focused on trying to calm Molly and helping set priorities for Rosie's care. Returning to the nursing facility was no longer an option. Molly would continue to care for Rosie in her home and we discussed ways to help her feel better being there. We talked about how we could treat various symptoms, how we could adjust some medications and how really, what mattered at this point was the quality of Rosie's life. After that visit, I called Molly several times to continue offering support and encouragement. Rosie had some good days and other days when she slept a lot.

It turned out that those were the last weeks of Rosie's life. She died in her sleep several weeks later. The last time I saw her was at her wake, in a room full of people who told stories and shared happy memories, celebrating and honoring her life.

It was a humbling experience to know that my medical interventions were not central in the end. Listening and empathy were the best medicine. And in that action, Rosie and Molly gave back to me by trusting me and letting me into their last days together. Being able to take care of her, I felt like a family member.

Sitting with them

Cherita Raines

Mr. W was living his life, feeling fine. He used the machine that benefits many people with sleep apnea use, a continuous positive airway pressure, or CPAP machine. One night when plugging in his CPAP, he broke the humerus bone in his arm. He was admitted to his nearby hospital, and on the operating table, the surgeons discovered that his fracture was from a tumor. The cancer had spread to his arm from somewhere else in his body. Without a clear origin, he was sent from his home in Alaska to our regional Veterans Hospital (the "VA") for further evaluation. That was about 6 weeks before I met him. He became "my" patient; I was five months into my internship, doing a medicine rotation at the VA.

It seemed appropriate that we were heading into the Christmas holiday season when he arrived at our hospital and I met him and his wife. Mr. W was quick to joke that he often played Santa Claus because he was so rotund. My first job was to hear his story and do his physical exam. Then we had the "code status" discussion. Would he want to be resuscitated, with CPR and medications, if his heart stopped? If he got very ill and needed help breathing, would he want to be intubated if necessary? Because the nature of his cancer was undefined at that time, Mr. W and his wife decided that he would be "full code," allowing full resuscitation attempts if needed. I put those orders in the chart where I also put the written record of the history I obtained and the results of my physical exam.

Day two of his hospitalization: the CT scan of his chest and abdomen showed his liver and his ribs full of tumors. He had metastatic cancer. Seeing those films, I felt a big lump in my throat and my heart sank. Mr. W would not have long to live, and I had to tell him. We would also need to discuss reversing his code status to "Do Not Resuscitate." I was not looking forward to the sad conversations we faced.

My senior resident took the lead. She told Mr. W and his wife what the CT scan showed. She recommended changing his code status to "Do Not Resuscitate" because chest compressions would break his ribs and guarantee a very painful, traumatic death. While she was talking, I watched Mr. and

Mrs. W. They had initially been smiling, but now he stared straight ahead and his smile was gone. After a moment, Mrs. W's face relaxed, she looked at her husband, grabbed his hand, and said "it's okay; you will be okay," and her smile returned. Mr. W. looked into her eyes and his face relaxed to her reassuring words.

Later that day the oncology team reviewed the CT scan and considering his widespread cancer, they determined he was not a candidate for any curative treatment. We could offer him palliative and hospice care. I was sure he would want to be cared for in his home.

Mr. W was off having another test done, but I knew they would want to know the decisions of the oncology team before I left for the day. I went to Mr. W's room and talked with his wife about palliative and hospice care, hopefully back in Alaska, in their home. She said she understood and would pass the message on to her husband when he got back to his room. I asked her if there was anything that I could do for them. She thanked me for all of our help and she had two requests.

"While he is here for the next few days, he would really like to have a room to himself, because he likes to sing. He often sings around the house back home." She also asked that her husband be able to speak to their eldest son. They had not seen him for some time because he was deployed in the military. I did not get him the private room in time for singing, but our team assistant began the process to locate their son and obtain permission for leave to come to see his father.

Day three was a Friday. I returned to work in the morning to find a note at my desk telling me to call military personnel staff. When I called, I was asked, "How sick is Mr. W? And is he expected to die soon and if so, how soon?" I thought there would be time for Mr. W to return home to Alaska, but wanted to make sure that his son saw his father again. "Put him on the next plane" was my response. Next on my list was to see how quickly we could set up hospice and fly Mr. W back home.

On morning rounds, Mr. W was in good spirits, looking forward to leaving. By the end of that Friday, we got confirmation that that their son was coming the next day, Saturday, and a flight back to Alaska was scheduled for Sunday. That same day, Mr. W spoke with his other son over the phone. And the biopsy results were back: esophageal adenocarcinoma, a cancer in his esophagus that had spread. I gave Mrs. W a hug before leaving work that evening. This was a devastating diagnosis, but we could at least feel good that some things had fallen into place. He was going home and hospice was going to meet them at their house. Mr. W would see his eldest son, and would not spend the holidays in this hospital.

Day four was Saturday morning, and before I could put my coffee down a nurse paged me to come immediately to Mr. W's bedside. Mr. W had oxygen prongs in his nose and was gasping for air, his eyes wide with panic, in respiratory distress. The respiratory therapist's attempt to suction Mr. W's throat provided no relief. Was the tumor in his esophagus bleeding into his lungs, or maybe closing off his airway? At that moment, the cause was less important than providing some relief. Turning to the nurse, I asked for a "stat" order of Ativan to calm Mr. W, and to see if he could be moved to a private room. I was concerned that his wife was not yet at the bedside, that he was alone. I silently hoped she got there soon.

I explained to Mr. W what was happening and told him about the medications to help calm him and his breathing. He nodded as his wife entered the room. I walked up to her and said, "Given what is happening now, he may not live through today." She started crying and when I hugged her, she whispered in my ear, "What am I supposed to do? He gave me 35 great years."

"Go and tell him just that," I responded.

After a few minutes without improvement, I asked them both if I could switch him over to comfort care and start a morphine drip. "The drip will help you to be comfortable," I told him, having also to add, "and it is also possible that it will hasten death. Your son might not get here before you die."

He was sleepy from the Ativan, and she took no time to decide. "Please start the drip. I want my husband to be as comfortable as possible. Our son will understand."

I wrote the order and Mr. W was moved to a private room when the morphine drip was started.

After seeing my other patients and writing daily progress notes, my supervising doctor told me to sign out my patients to the on-call team and go home. The doctors "on call" cover their patients and the patients of the doctors who are going "off call," handling any problems and decisions that come up during the time that a patent's regular doctor is off. I signed out all of my other patients, but not Mr. W. I could have gone home, but I thought to myself, "What do I have to do for the rest of the day? Catch up on shows that were in my DVR?" Leaving did not seem right.

I took off my white coat and went to Mr. W's room. It was quiet. Mr. W was asleep, breathing with less difficulty, the morphine doing its job. His eyes were shut and the muscles in his face relaxed. I pulled up a chair next to Mrs. W, grabbed her hand, and said, "Tell me about the first time you two met." She let out a small chuckle, shook her head from side to side, her face instantly showing her going back to that time. She asked me if Mr. W could hear her. I said I believed yes, and she began their story. It was 10:30am.

She regaled me with stories of their dates and the secret hand signal she would give him at parties to let him know that his right eye was wandering and that he needed to concentrate so that he would not look cross-eyed. She told me about how he had such a wonderful singing voice and strong lungs that made him a great swimmer. I sat there, holding her hand, wishing I had more time to get to know Mr. W better.

Around 1pm Mr. W's breathing became more infrequent. Their son arrived and I stepped out to give him and his mother some time alone with Mr. W.

After a short while, the son called me back into the room. We sat, the three of us, sometimes talking and sometimes silent. Mr. W's breathing became more and more infrequent. His wife went up to him and whispered in his ear, "It's okay, we will be okay, you can let go." About twenty minutes later, I walked up to Mr. W and placed my stethoscope to his chest for the last time. Time to heaven: 2:13pm.

That day I learned that doctoring happens to the end: sometimes, the best thing we can do as a physician is to be present. As a friend or family member, it is the same. Being with this family during this time reminded me about being present to what is happening in life and about the importance of making memories of my own. When my time comes to leave this earth, I want someone to be able to share hours of wonderful stories about me.

Anatomy of Caring
Sharon Dobie

I have known Lisa since she was a pre-teen and I was her mother's doctor. I have known her sister just as long. Initially I was just her mother's doctor. In those years, knowing Lisa and her sister was only through her mother's renditions of their lives, usually through the lens of maternal worries. I saw her and her sister a few times as teens and young adults and then they would disappear off my list of regular patients. I did not deliver Lisa's children and never met them or her husband until the next generation were teens. After years when I only cared for her mother, more of this family has migrated to my care. Now I am Lisa's doctor, her mother's doctor, and the doctor for her husband, her children, and her mother-in-law.

Our visits always start with a hug. Not all my visits with my patients start this way. With this family, we feel a kinship that warrants a hug. They are comfortable with that and so am I.

What I know about them and their lives is through the stories offered during our visits. I know how well Lisa's kids are doing in school and their aspirations. I know her husband's medical challenges and how he did not like being stuck at home after surgery. I commiserate with her about how she cannot control whether or not her mother-in-law takes her medication and I support the relationship she has with her mother, who lives with too much pain. I refill pain medications for the matriarch, treat viruses and ear infections for the younger kids, work on health screenings for all members of the family, and support and advise Lisa, who tries to manage life for everyone.

Hopefully I help this family as their physician. What I know is that, like others in this chapter, I feel just a little less invisible, more real because we are in each other's lives. Simultaneous with my care for them, they follow my life as a mother, doctor, friend, and family member, and the ups and downs we have had. There are no illusions that any one of us is somehow perfect, and they never ask me to be above and removed from them, or somehow without flaws. Their acceptance of me and me of them is glue in the bond between us. In the elusive anatomy of caring, authenticity might be the backbone that allows the doctor-patient relationship to be a relationship.

Physicians (maybe patients too) don't talk much about what results from the wealth of exposure that comes from being invited into our patients' lives. From this place we witness and share, and our lives co-mingle. As they and we live, handling difficulties and facing joys, challenges, and death, how could we not be affected? The following four chapters on joy, hope, courage, and dying all reflect on what happens when we are part of a patient's life, close enough to observe and participate, and close enough to learn about ourselves.

Chapter 2

Cheer in Our Midst

Hatman and the Royal Typewriter
Sharon Dobie

"A Mr. Dorfel is waiting to see you," paged our clinic receptionist. I was finishing notes from my morning clinic, but went out to greet him in our empty waiting room. As soon as he saw me, he jumped up, same plaid flannel shirt, dentures clacking, toupee askew, and wrapped me in a big hug, almost dropping the several rubber-banded bundles of papers clutched in his hand. "Dr. D, we need to talk."

Though I had not seen him for several years, Hugh and I went way back. He had been my patient at Country Doctor Community Health Centers, and he briefly followed me to the university medical center when I left the clinic and changed jobs. When the university billing style and increased cost became more than he cared to manage, he had returned to the community health center for his medical care.

When I was his doctor at the health center, our relationship had a rhythm: six months (summer and fall) of fairly frequent visits for his high blood pressure and preventive care, and six months (winter and spring) of absence when he would escape to Mexico for its lower cost of living and warm winters. When he would return, his line was the same: "Dr. D, I would stay there all the year, but as you know, yours truly cannot take that heat. And Seattle is dandy, but on that medicine you give me, my hands are just too cold for the winters here. And Mexico is just marvelously, wonderfully inexpensive," he said, drawing out "marvelously" like someone from the Upper West Side describing last night's gala.

His absences were punctuated by long, rambling, usually tangential letters to me, handwritten or typed on the old Royal typewriter that he hauled back and forth between Mexico and Seattle. He wrote on the politics of the day, his days in Mexico, my doctoring, stories he read in the *New York Times*, and other topics on his mind. A diehard liberal and pacifist, he always tucked several *New Yorker* cartoons into the envelopes carrying his letters, which were hard to read in his scrawling hand and sprawling grammar. We would pass the letters around the clinic, and with laughter and delight, my co-workers and I would take turns at trying to decipher the handwriting and to translate the run-on sentences into a comprehensible message. We all knew another autumn would bring Hugh back to the clinic, stopping at each person's desk, complimenting everyone he encountered.

When he was in Seattle and still had his apartment, he took the bus across town every day to the post office where he kept his P.O. box. This way, he said, he could run into all his old friends all over town. They included the bus driver, the regulars on the city bus, and the checkers in his favorite grocery store, where he bought bags of fresh vegetables and grains every day for cooking in his pressure cooker. He befriended everyone. He would say, "If I can make someone's day brighter, why not?" He often told me what a good person I was, whether he was considering me as a doctor, a mother, or just as a human being, and he was similarly generous with pretty much everyone he met along the way.

One of his favorite refrains about his health went something like this: "You know, I should be dead. When I was thirty-five, that one doctor told me that I would be dead by the time I was forty. It's that high blood pressure of mine, through the roof, but I told him it's had always been that way. And you know it still is that way. It's just me, blood pressure always bouncing all over the place. And here I am, still kicking. Who would have imagined?"

Yes, each fall, he would appear, each year getting closer to 80, his toupee even more bedraggled than the year before, possessing few worldly goods and reasonably good health other than his high blood pressure and formerly enlarged prostate, which he loved to tell any listening audience was the largest his surgeon had ever removed. We would listen to his critical monologues about the state of the world and peppered with his belief in the goodness of some people in government. There he was again each year, asking after each staff member's and my children's health with many repetitions of "and give my hearty best to them."

Most of us doctors have some optimists among those we treat. How many of these patients know their effect on us? My clinic day is scheduled with appointments every few minutes. A first look at the schedule before starting a clinic gives me a sense of the patients I will be seeing. Sometimes that glance can open a floodgate of feelings ranging from anxiety about not knowing enough, to distress when seeing a challenging patient on the schedule, to delight at certain other names on the list. Some patients, like Hugh, quite simply brighten my day. These patients are just as likely as others to have major illnesses, and as you will see in the following stories, some of them were dying when the authors worked with them. Yet even when there are trials or death, some individuals experience life in ways that transcend what is difficult, and they share that spirit with everyone around them.

Standing at Her Door

Ted Carter

As a senior resident in pediatrics thirty years ago, I took care of a little girl with acute myelogenous leukemia (AML). That was the time of 100-hour-plus work weeks for residents, and while I was neither disillusioned nor second-guessing my career choice, I was tired, worn out, and aware that getting up each morning to go to the hospital was not exactly fun.

The 2-year-old girl with AML was ill but stable when she was admitted to the hospital. Julie's parents had noticed that she was bruising easily and getting paler. A blood count test had demonstrated findings suspicious for leukemia, and she was admitted to our hematology-oncology service to do further tests and to start treatment. In her room she played happily, babbling and cheerful. Most toddlers get wary of the doctors and staff who poke and prod and approach them with needles, but Julie was different. Even though there were many needle sticks, she never seemed to shy away from us in fear. She tired easily and when she was not up playing with toys, she would be in her bed or in her parents' arms asleep.

She went though a bone marrow biopsy, where we take a sample of bone marrow by piercing the bone with a large needle. It was a drawn out, painful procedure, for which she only had local anesthesia. I felt sorrow for the pain we were causing and frustration and concern over how many times we needed to ram that needle into her bone to get enough of a marrow sample. Julie whimpered but did not cry out, and she held still. It amazed me that she never complained, or even expressed anger or fear towards us after what we had done to her.

This engaging, curly-haired girl remained in the hospital throughout my month-long rotation. She was in isolation, so she never left her room. Each morning she would stand at her door talking, waving, and smiling. Soon I realized that I was looking forward to each day. I actually wanted to get up and go to the hospital. From her doorway, this little girl had changed my approach to the day and rekindled my love of my work.

Julie went into remission, went home, relapsed, and then went into remission again. She suffered through many treatments and complications. I lost touch with her but remembered her, until approximately two years later when she was hospitalized with a severe pneumonia from varicella, the virus that causes chicken pox. I became her doctor again. She had to be intubated and on the ventilator and although she survived that illness, she relapsed again with her AML. Chemotherapy was started again because this was before the advent of bone marrow transplants.

Weakened from the pneumonia and then from the chemotherapy, she lay in her bed and showed less interest in her toys or us. She cried more and laughed less during those months, yet she always had a smile for the staff.

She died during that hospitalization. I felt that the world had lost a shining light, though I also felt relief that her pain and suffering had ended. My grief at her death never obscured my memory of her as a bright ray of sunshine illuminating dreary days. How can one be so happy and giving at such a young age and under such duress? That is still a mystery to me, but some of us, and many children, possess such gifts. She, and other children for whom I have cared during my many years in medicine, taught me a bit about taking setbacks in stride, enjoying the little things, and living each day one at a time. She taught me how to be happy amidst tragedy and how to see triumph in what appears to be failure – a true gift.

Self-Acceptance
Reiko Johnson

Margaret, a 50-year old woman with end-stage liver disease from alcoholism, has been on the transplant list for a year and a half. I took care of her once when I was a resident where she was hospitalized, and now she sees me in my family medicine clinic. Margaret had been her mother's caregiver for years – a role that seemed to conspire with her alcoholism in leading her to neglect her own health. But despite everything, she comes to appointments now with many focused and articulate questions that show an emerging interest in her health. Clearly strong in resolve and determination, she quit drinking and almost quit smoking to prepare for a transplant. She laughs a lot, often poking fun at herself. She also asks me about myself, showing an interest in me as a person training as a resident. She seems grounded, happy, and fulfilled.

Nothing seems to faze her. Margaret may die from this disease, yet I never sense that she feels sorry for herself or that she regrets the life she chose to live. Instead she brings laughter and self-acceptance to our visits. I laugh easily with her, and although she has many medical problems, she often "makes my clinic day" because visiting with her is so easy and joyful. A sense of humor and dignity can survive even serious illness and misfortune. When I am stressed, I remember Margaret and that lesson, and am enriched.

Smiles

Reiko Johnson

I like the small smiles Mr. P gives me. He has diabetes, heart failure, and kidney disease, in addition to alcoholism. He is a man of very few words and I cannot always read his emotions, but his smiles convey his appreciation of me, and I look forward to seeing him. His sister does most of the talking for him about his health. She sits close to him, holds his hand, and frequently looks to him as if to see if he agrees with what she tells me. Even though he doesn't say much, I sense that he thinks no one has really cared for him the way I do, and that he and his sister appreciate my efforts. The connection I feel with patients like him makes the hard work I do worthwhile. A small smile: enough.

His Eyes
Reiko Johnson

He was only seven when he died in his sleep and we were heartbroken. During his short life he smiled all the time, brightening up the room with his presence. He had severe cerebral palsy and communicated mostly with his eyes and his laughter. Everyone loved to just sit with him, talk to him, and make him laugh. Back then, I was a volunteer coordinator for a non-profit organization serving disabled and seriously ill children and their brothers and sisters. I liked to hang out at the office with dozens of kids and volunteers.

He was really loved by his mom and all of us at the organization, and my heart would melt when he smiled. He couldn't speak words and he didn't have control of his movements, but that didn't seem to matter to him or to the rest of us who adored him. He communicated so much with his eyes, mouth, neck, whole body.

Some would judge this boy's quality of life to have been poor – at age 7 he functioned like an infant. But I believe he was truly a happy soul, and his contribution to the world was touching people in positive ways. We all break out in smiles when we think about him. I miss him.

Brightening Our Days
Sharon Dobie

I find pleasure in both the science of my work and the very human relationships I have with patients. Those who bring optimism to their appointments are contagious, softening the exam room by creating an atmosphere that crowds out the worry, grief, and irritations of the day. Maria and Clara come to mind immediately. They don't know each other, yet they share the capacity to brighten my day.

Maria comes in once a month. A few years ago she had a small stroke; she recovered fully and needs to take warfarin, a blood thinner, to prevent another stroke. Patients taking warfarin must have their blood checked monthly, which creates an opportunity for Maria to pop in to review her blood test results. She is an active septuagenarian who does volunteer work, travels, reads, and follows current events. Usually our short visits include my asking a few questions to make sure she is not silently bleeding (from excessive blood thinning) or having stroke symptoms. They also include her political narratives peppered with raucous sarcasm. When Bush invaded Iraq she was worried and dismayed; when Obama was nominated and then elected, she was elated. As a state employee I am not allowed to discuss partisan politics, but we both know this part of her visit is as much for me as for her. When we part, I wonder if she understands that I am grateful for spending those enjoyable minutes with her.

At the age of 94, Clara lives alone. Years ago she rejected her daughters' advice to hire someone to help clean the house. "In my opinion, it is clean enough," she told me, and then laughed, a contagious, out-loud laugh.

She had open-heart surgery last year and afterwards Clara, like Maria, had to take the blood thinner warfarin for a number of months. That meant her laughter filled our exam room one day each month when she came to check her lab values. At one point, having forgotten the precise dose of a medicine another doctor gave her, she said, laughing again, "You should charge me more for my forgetfulness." Now that she is no longer taking the warfarin, I probably will see her only a few times a year. I am weaning myself from her frequent visits and her laughter, hoping I remember how good it feels to laugh as much and as out loud as Clara does.

Hatman Celebrations
Sharon Dobie

This chapter ends as it started: with Hugh. When he appeared, unannounced, that day in my clinic, I had not seen him for probably two years. I took him out to lunch. "Doctor Sharon, I need you to be the executor of my will," he said, handing me a card from one of his rubber-banded bunches of papers. "I have this attorney and she says I need to name someone. I don't have anything to do with my kids, and I can't ask my apartment manager even though she's a great gal. You're the only one who can do this. It should not be any work. Really."

From there he rambled on about his latest six months in Mexico, how his blood pressure was doing, and the health and welfare of the my former co-workers at the community health center. "And how are the boys, Mr. Matthew and Mr. Nicholas?" he asked me, always attentive to hearing how my family was faring. During his loquacious monologue he polished off his bowl of hot and sour soup and didn't press me to grant his request. I asked him to meet me again in a week.

Though it had been years since I had been Hugh's doctor, I knew his social situation. He had never revealed details about why he was estranged from his son and daughter and he sidestepped any of my attempts to suggest that he think about reconciling with them. At our next lunch, I agreed conditionally to his request that I be his executor, telling him, "This can only work if you stay in touch. I cannot have you here or in Mexico and have no idea where you are or how you're doing."

He dutifully stayed in touch, with those long letters when he was in Mexico and coffee dates when he was in town. After several years, Hugh's health declined. I helped him find assisted living and his Mexico jaunts ended; my sons got to know him better and he became a more like a member of our family. We would visit him and he would come to our house for special occasions. Several hospitalizations and a number of years later, he moved to a skilled nursing facility where he lived until he died.

During this final period of his life, Hugh, now in his eighties, became the hat man. In his sixties and seventies, he had worn a toupee that became increasingly dirty and matted. During one hospitalization, his nurse supported my ultimatum: "lose the wig and be happily bald, or buy a new wig. This one's a rat's nest and is going in the garbage." He gave up the toupee and replaced it with hats, often flamboyant or funny ones. In the nursing home he started accumulating baseball caps, beanies, and hats for special occasions: a witch's hat, a leprechaun's hat, a Santa hat, a pinwheel hat. On my visits, I often would find him, up to three hats on his head at a time, sitting in his wheelchair by the nursing station. Smiling at the nurse, he would tell me, "This is my friend, Martha, and she works so hard and is the best nurse here." Later he would confide, "We need to show more appreciation for the staff here. They work so hard, and people are always complaining."

This man brought a smile to my face whether I was seeing him in clinic, reading one of his quirky, barely understandable letters, picturing him heading across town to get his mail or across continents to Mexico, watching him interact with nursing home residents and staff, or sitting at my dining room table. Though he would have virtually no money when he died, his wish was to give his little reserve fund to the health center where he received care for over 20 years. I convinced him to give it to them while he was still alive and took him to a clinic staff meeting for the presentation. To their standing ovation, he told them "You work so hard, too hard, and I want you to have some time to just relax." His gift was to the staff and earmarked specifically to fund staff parties. He wanted them to remember to celebrate.

Chapter 3

Courage

Living While He Could
Sharon Dobie

"We've decided to go ahead."

"Tell me about it," I asked.

Having come together to this appointment, this young couple was sitting side by side in one of our exam rooms, holding hands and looking at each other. Neither was smiling, and his free hand stroked their joined hands. Having met with them separately and together while they considered their options, this was not our first conversation about this decision.

Rick was a visual artist and musician who also worked as a house painter. Ann was an accountant for a medium-sized firm. They had met, had a fairly whirlwind romance, married, bought a little house, and were looking forward to having a couple of children. In the months before I knew them, Rick started to notice some odd things about his body. He thought his grip on the paintbrush was weakening, and his coordination seemed a bit off. Then his step grew less sure on the ladders propped against the houses he was painting. At first he thought it was fatigue. But his symptoms did not get better, and a tremor developed. He kept all this to himself, not liking to make a fuss, and liking doctors even less. Eventually Ann noticed.

They were in their early thirties when I met them. ALS (Amyotrophic Lateral Sclerosis, Lou Gehrig's disease) had entered their lives. This poorly understood condition has no cure. The cells that communicate with and make up the motor nerve fibers begin to degenerate, and neurons deteriorate and die. The brain then cannot start or control muscle movement. It is a relentless condition with no predictable course. Some people live many years in a slow decline; for others it is fatal within a few years.

I met them because Ann was the sister-in-law of a colleague, Keith, who said they needed a family doctor in addition to the specialists Rick would be seeing. Keith approached me with a clear picture of what my role should be for this family: "They will need someone to oversee his care. More importantly, they will need someone who will be honest with them as they deal with Rick's changing health and with the tough decisions that will accompany those changes." Cane or no cane (yet)? Wheelchair? Special implements for eating? Feeding tube? A ventilator? Treat pneumonia after respiratory function is severely compromised? These were questions we all knew Rick and his family would face, but hopefully not for many years. Whether to have or not have a child was one of the first big questions this couple tackled with me.

From my conversations with them I could picture them at home: late nights, long talks at the kitchen table, couch, or in bed, sifting through facts and emotions, many tears. Despite all their talking and some magical thinking, they could not exorcise the reality in their midst—ALS. What was certain: it is a fatal disease. What was uncertain: did he have two years or ten or more to live? They still had to reconcile that with their yearnings for children.

They raised the question about having children soon after our first meeting, knowing that if they wanted a child, now was going to be better than later, and knowing it was a complex decision for them. Should they go forward if one parent has a high likelihood of dying before his child graduates from high school?"

In Ann's early conversations, alone with me, her face was tight, lips barely moving, eyes initially dry. "I am young. I am so angry about this. This is not what I wanted, for Christ's sake, not for him, not for me." She would move quickly from that anger to wondering if it was selfish to want a baby, both for them and for a part of Rick to live on. She would ask the pragmatic question: did she want to bear the burden of parenting when Rick became too disabled to even hold their child, and of eventually becoming a single parent?

Rick struggled to find the middle position between feelings: selfish if they went forward and angrily cheated if they did not, and he always landed in that third ever-present domain of not wanting to be a burden to others.

I understood the ambivalence in their feelings. As a single person

I adopted first one and then another baby. I wanted to be a parent and decided not to wait for a partner. They were decisions that felt right, if not a completely rational. I too had worries about the "what ifs." What if something happens to me? What if I can't really do this on my own? What if this is not fair to the children? There were also a few raised eyebrows in my social circle. Working with Rick and Ann, I wondered what proportion of their discussions felt to them as "makes sense" and what proportion seemed "a little crazy." Choosing to have a child was so right for their stage of life and yet, given Rick's illness, they had to feel it was outside of the realm of the purely rational. On the other hand, is that decision ever completely rational? And for anyone, what is the stuff of that kind of decision? Is it blindness? Faith? A dash of hope? Biologic determinism? Maybe a bit of courage?

Eventually they decided. "We don't know how long Rick will live," Ann said, "but we want to live fully in the time we have. Having children is what we have always wanted. So we will try to get pregnant and we will see where it takes us."

"I worry about leaving Ann alone with our child, if I die in a few years," Rick added. "I thought it was a selfish thing to do to a kid, having him come into a family where one person is going to die." With a shrug of his shoulders, he added, "Then again, we think we will be pretty cool parents, and who's to say I won't get lucky and live a lot of years?"

"OK then," I said. What else was there to say, after having discussed Rick's illness, their support systems, and the pros and cons of starting a family when one parent has a degenerative disease?

Ann got pregnant fairly quickly. After normal genetic screening, a remarkably normal pregnancy, and a few harrowing moments during her labor a week or so past her due date, she delivered a healthy son. She and Rick left the hospital for home less than 24 hours after their son's birth.

Ann returned to work after her maternity leave, and Rick was able to stay home caring for their son. He painted a mural covering one entire side of their garage, turning their small back yard into a dream world for a child's and whole family's imagination. On warm days they played in that space; on cold or rainy ones, the mural was visible from their indoor play-space. As his son grew through babyhood, Rick's illness progressed more rapidly than anyone anticipated. They faced the mobility assistance needs, feeding tube and ventilator options, and other major decisions one at a time, never letting Rick's illness define them or constrict them prematurely. In the space where they created a family, they lived until Rick died. Their son was two years old.

What is it about the human spirit that keeps us going in the face of whatever challenges there are? What creates that day-to-day grit to get up and face both the ordinary and extraordinary? Less about the "how," what seems more important is the commonality that people usually do keep going – just plain do keep going.

I watch my patients live their lives, and whether there is success or even motivation is really not the point. I see a broad range of possible ways to face and cope with what is in front of us, whether it is opportunity or difficulty. As the following stories illustrate, physicians all, knowingly or unknowingly, become students in this experiential classroom. We are exposed to the ways that people act and give meaning and shape to words like courage, beyond what we reserve for the famous and more blatantly heroic. That exposure can change us.

Hoodie

Kavitha Chunchu

It was another clinic day, and I was moving down my schedule at a decent pace for a change. My next patient, a 31-year-old woman, was listed as a "Follow Up from Walk-In Clinic/ Diabetes/ Headaches." Prior to entering the room, I looked through the notes from that walk-in clinic visit. She was diagnosed with diabetes, headaches, blepharitis (eyelid inflammation), and a urinary tract infection, and she was started on an antibiotic. I thought, "Wow, a lot of diagnoses for one visit!"

In the exam room a young woman, close to my age, was sitting on the examination table wearing a green sweatshirt with the hood up. She introduced me to her sister, who was sitting near the wall.

The patient had some very obvious swelling around both eyes. As we chatted about her prior clinic visit and her newly diagnosed diabetes, she said that her eye swelling had been present for a week. She also told me about her headaches. Her blood test results from the walk-in clinic visit showed a white blood cell count of 15, the normal being under 10. Did she have an infection? I also noticed our medical assistant had documented a rapid pulse. Things were not adding up, and I was beginning to get a little confused. What was really going on with this young woman?

Because of her eye swelling and headaches, I wanted to perform a thorough HEENT (Head, Eye, Ear, Nose, and Throat) exam. So after the usual pre-exam ritual of bathing my hands in sanitizing alcohol gel, I asked her to push back the hood of her sweatshirt. That simple request was not based on any special insight of mine; it was simply based on my training: I needed to see the part of the body I wanted to examine. I certainly did not expect it to become a turning point in our visit.

The patient asked her sister to leave the room for the exam, and then she began to cry. I asked her what was wrong. She said, "I don't want to scare her." She moved back the hood of her sweatshirt. On the top of her head was a large, plum–sized, fluctuant red mass, clearly an abscess, a boil. The scalp looked thin, so this abscess was tense with fluid, likely pus. It was doubtless very painful, maybe the source of her headaches and swollen eyes. "I have been so scared to tell anyone because I am afraid that I have a tumor," she said as she continued to cry. She had not shown this to the doctor in urgent care.

So many thoughts were going through my mind at this point. At first I thought, "Oh shit." This thought was a mixture of disbelief and sorrow that she had been dealing with this condition alone. I told myself, "Do not show that you are shocked; how you react next is going to matter." So I held her hand and told her, "I appreciate how much courage it took for you to overcome those fears and come in to see me. It is really important that you showed me this. And it is not a tumor!"

Medically, from my standpoint, the next things that occurred were pretty routine. She was admitted to the hospital for imaging (getting a picture of size and how deeply the abscess went), intravenous antibiotics, and incision and drainage of the abscess, which turned out to be limited to her scalp, not invading bone.

Almost two weeks later, I found out that she was discharged from the hospital and came back to clinic for a follow-up visit with her primary care provider (PCP). Her eye swelling, headaches, and her diabetes had improved. She admitted to her doctor that she almost refused to bring down her hood that day in clinic. She waited for a few minutes to say hello to me after her office visit, but I was in a room with another patient and she left. She told her PCP she would try to see me next time. I am looking forward to seeing her.

Looking back, I am moved by the simple act of this woman removing her hood. What made her take it off? Why at that moment? Was she just tired of hurting? Was she ready to confront her own fears? What changed in her life or her internal conversation that gave her this strength? I wish I knew the answers to those questions. She literally and metaphorically took down a barrier in order to allow me to see what was happening. She could have decided, as she did at the walk-in clinic, to keep her secret hidden. However, afraid of cancer, afraid about what would happen next, she still allowed her vulnerability and her fears to be on display to a stranger. She trusted or needed something in our encounter enough to allow her to share.

I will remember this woman for a long time. It's easy to assume that in the doctor's office patients will readily share what is really happening. That is the purpose of coming to see a doctor, right? When patients cry in the examination room, I always tell them, "If you can't cry with your doctor, who can you cry with?" But this story will remind me that asking for help can be unbelievably difficult—that our fears prevent us from making changes or reaching out. What I expect from patients – the ability, willingness, and courage to share something painful or scary – is not something I easily do myself in my personal life. I pride myself on being an autonomous individual, probably to a fault. I rarely ask for and I decline offers for help. My "can-do" spirit probably adds to my tendency to resist letting people in. Though I can't say that this woman's actions have brought down my own walls, they have helped me recognize my struggles about sharing my vulnerabilities and they give me a deeper appreciation of what we ask our patients to do: to open their needs and hurts to us.

Stepping Over Fear
Sharon Dobie

"Will you please be my doctor? I am changing insurance plans and need a new doctor. I will tell you up front, I do not examine my own breasts. I am terrified to do so. My mother had breast cancer at a young age. So did a cousin. My sister had ovarian cancer. I get mammograms every year, but I want to come to the doctor every four months for a breast exam."

That was the beginning of our patient-doctor relationship. She is an active professional, friend, wife, and mother in her sixties, and clearly at high risk for getting breast cancer. There are many responses she could have to this risk. For her the risk brings fear, but she manages it through having the courage to choose what feels like a decent coping strategy. She lives with fear and courage together.

It's reassuring that my patients usually find a way to carry on, even when the challenge seems paralyzing, and I am oddly strengthened by our time together. If she can carry on through her fear, well then, so can I. Thinking back, when my mother was ill I kept working, faced my fears and, despite how I felt, did not crawl under the covers and hide from what was happening. As I examine the breasts of my patient and once again tell her I find nothing of concern, I think about her life and mine. I still cannot quite answer the question, "how do we manage to do this?"

The Tended Garden
Sharon Dobie

Alena had been a housewife for many years. She and John, a retired pharmacy tech, were remarkably devoted to each other. I never saw or heard an irritated look or tone of voice from either of them when talking to or about one another. At times I secretly wondered if there was more to their relationship, maybe carefully hidden by the story they presented to me. The only possible candidate for "more to the story" was that they were estranged from their children for religious reasons. Alena's and John's faith was so strong that they would not see or communicate with their children who had left their church.

They loved to garden. Herbs were their specialty, and each summer clinic staff and I eagerly anticipated their visits. Alena and John would arrive with large grocery bags of bundled herbs that filled our waiting room with the scents of rosemary, thyme, lavender, basil, mustards, and mints until they were divided among most of us working in our clinic.

Alena had diabetes and severe coronary artery disease. By the time I met her, she had already had three heart attacks and had four vessels bypassed ("CABG" or coronary artery bypass grafting). More of her coronary arteries had blockages, and because they were in the smaller branching vessels, they could not be made better with either stents or bypassing. She worked hard to control her blood sugar with diet and medications, and she dutifully took other medications for her heart, cholesterol, and kidneys. Nevertheless, recurrent bouts of chest pain continued to plague her, those small areas of her heart muscle hurting from the inadequate oxygen poorly supplied by partially blocked vessels.

Over time, less and less activity would lead to chest pains. Even walking across the yard would bring them on. Yet she often said, "If I can be in the garden, I'm happy." They bought a wheel chair and she would scoot around the garden, doing the chair-high pruning and harvesting.

During one period a few years before she died, she was hospitalized almost monthly with chest pain. The standard home protocol was not working. Her husband would give her sublingual nitroglycerine for the pain, and if it did not subside he could repeat it two more times. If by the third dose the pain did not stop, they were supposed to come to the hospital. We would admit her, given her medicine and oxygen, do electrocardiograms, and check her cardiac enzymes to see if there was death of heart muscle signaling another heart attack. When her pain resolved and we knew she had not had a heart attack, she would go home.

After four or five identical events she and John sat me down. "I don't want to keep coming to the hospital," she said. "You don't do anything for me. Even if I have a heart attack, no operation can fix this. So why am I coming to the hospital?"

"Well," I paused. "I guess the main point is we can give you oxygen to hopefully get more of it to your heart even if the vessels are not transporting it so well. Maybe that way we prevent a heart attack in that part of your heart muscle. Also we can give you medication to dilate the vessels. We have to watch your blood pressure, because those meds can lower your blood pressure dangerously. And we can give you morphine for the pain." Although I knew these things were little to offer, I added, "And if you had a large heart attack, you would be in the hospital where we can take care of you, hopefully stabilize things." I think we all knew saying "stabilize things" for her during a big heart attack was pretty euphemistic.

"Why can't I do that at home?" she asked, watching John, who was nodding along with her words.

I did not have a good answer for them, feeling caught between what seemed actually reasonable when I thought about it and something that seemed risky and not something I had done before. In fact, we weren't doing much for her in the hospital. They pressed me to give them what they needed for treatment at home and I finally agreed. The three of us worked out guidelines that addressed when to give oxygen, when to give morphine and how much, how to monitor her blood pressure in addition to her pulse, and when to call us or 9-1-1. They went home with medicines, syringes, and an oxygen tank. Her bouts of pain continued, but clinic visits and our treatment plan with phone check-ins worked. Though I remained nervous and vigilant, she never was readmitted to the hospital.

In a call about two years later, John opened with, "Alena is sleeping," adding, "actually she has been sleeping really hard for two days."

"What happened?" I did not hide my concern, and his nonchalance concerned me even more. His usual tactic was to call me the same day when there were any new symptoms. Chest pain, flu-like illness – whatever the symptom, he was religious about checking in with our nurses and me. When nitroglycerine and oxygen did not resolve a bout of pain, one or two doses of morphine did, and she was usually her old self the next day. This sleeping for two days was not typical for her. I felt really anxious while I waited for the rest of the story.

"She had a really strong bout of chest pain. She never got short of breath but she did get sweaty. I put her oxygen on and gave her the nitro-glycerin and it did not help, so I gave her morphine. That only helped a little.

"Then I told her we should call 9-1-1 and come to the hospital, like we all agreed, and she refused. She downright refused. She told me not to call you, just to give her more medicine. I waited until it was time and then gave her more morphine. She said the pain was easing. Her blood pressure was ok, so I gave her another nitro. Over the next couple of hours, she settled down, and after one more dose of morphine, she said the pain was gone and that she was really tired. She's been really tired since then. I think she had a heart attack. She's waking up to eat and use the bathroom, but just feels tired. Her breathing is not hard and her blood pressure and blood sugars are fine."

I took a deep breath; what was done was done. It sounded to me like maybe some little branch of her coronary artery was getting worse. Had it finally closed off completely? Was the small portion of heart muscle that had been hurting from inadequate blood flow now infarcted, dead tissue that would need to scar, but no longer need the closed-off blood supply? Or was she lying there with "the big one" about to hit?

"Please bring her in for us to evaluate what happened," I pleaded.

"No, she just wants to rest. I will call you again tomorrow."

Alena got stronger each day and a week later was up and moving around more than she had been before the event. Up until she died a couple of years later, she never again had chest pain. I suspect that she probably did in fact have a small heart attack, where that vessel that had been partially blocked for several years had completely closed off, resulting in the death of a small amount of heart muscle. That bit of muscle had given her all that pain when it was getting some but inadequate blood supply. After that she never needed the home oxygen or morphine.

They kept gardening and they kept praying. They talked about knowing her days were numbered. They stuck to their routines and kept things simple. A couple of years later, John came home from an errand one day and found Alena on the floor, deceased. There was no sign of struggle. It appeared she had been crossing the room with her walker and had fallen, probably from either a heart attack or an arrhythmia of her heart.

We miss the overflowing bags of herbs they brought throughout the growing season and we miss the couple that brought them, showing us a kind of strength as they accommodated to their physical limitations in ways that allowed them to flourish.

Doing What I Have to Do
Sharon Dobie

"I'm just so tired all the time," she said. "I think it's chasing those twins around all day."

She was in to see me about her diabetes, not about her fatigue, a development I hadn't expected. She'd lost weight, which pleased her, not necessarily me. She attributed the decline to some loss of appetite, and was happy to be slimmer. I began to get nervous when she admitted to having black and tarry stools, a reliable sign of something bleeding in the stomach or intestinal tract. The anemia I had begun to fear showed up in the lab test results. The EGD, or esophagogastroduodenoscopy, the procedure where doctors use a scope to look down the esophagus and into the stomach and duodenum, showed an ulcer. The ulcer was cancer.

Stomach cancer is a sobering diagnosis. On a phone visit, I asked about her feelings. She said she cried a bit. "I am just going to deal with it. That's all," she said. "What is the point of anything else? Am I going to just lie down and die? No!" She laughed. Her family rallied. She signed them up to help out. Someone took her to all her appointments. She just did what she had to do.

I had first met her in the grocery store. She became "my checker," laughing with me about politics, her union work, and children. Besides the three she had successfully raised by the time I met her, she was also raising two nieces and then adopted a boy, right when I was adopting one and then another son. Oh, the stories we shared in the checkout line and later, when she became my patient, in our clinic visits. She is a no-nonsense parent and became my informal parenting mentor, giving me advice often and freely, regardless of whether I asked for it.

Cancer was just another place she had to step up. Handle it. She went to a different health care system for her cancer care and kept in touch with messages, calls and an occasional visit. She is now on the other side of chemotherapy and surgery, hoping to stay disease free. She stepped up and kept on keeping on.

If I had a diagnosis as foreboding as hers, I wonder if I could smile when I saw my doctor, maintain a good front for family, and keep up with treatment and life. She is no longer my checker; I am still her doctor and know: she would be there to mentor me.

Trying
Reiko Johnson

Mr. H is a 45-year old homeless male with chronic pain, heroin addiction, and bipolar illness with psychotic features. He has been coming to his appointments despite his chaotic lifestyle, and he is polite at all times. He is always trying to get his life in order. He has plans to become clean and sober, get a job, and find a place to live. Sobriety doesn't always last very long, but he stays motivated, and despite his difficult situation, he maintains a positive attitude and keeps trying. He doesn't give up. He is an optimist. I am a resident physician, some days just getting by. I know more about perseverance and resilience thanks to Mr. H.

Death of a Child

Sharon Dobie

Before she was six months of age, Annie's baby stopped developing normally. Her eyes and smiles spoke volumes to her family and care givers, but she did not learn to sit alone, stand, walk, or talk.

This could be, but is not, a story about this little girl. It is about the little girl's mother, who became my patient when the little girl was about 6. Annie devoted her life to her daughter, her older child, and her husband. With round-the-clock care at home, they managed, but the toll on Annie was heavy. She was often unable to sleep, get out of the house, or exercise. Trips to shop or visit friends were timed with her daughter's needs.

Annie and her husband spent hours talking together and with their pediatrician about best options for their daughter. She had many hospitalizations for infections and eventually she needed a feeding tube for nutrition and a ventilator to help her breathe. There came a time when she was eight years old when they realized that more hospitalizations were not going to prolong their daughter's life. They knew it was time to stop aggressive interventions. The next time she had signs of an infection, they chose to treat her at home and not to hospitalize her. She died shortly thereafter, eight and a half years old.

How does one find the strength to make such a decision? With that loss, how does one muster what it takes to continue living? After this child's death, how will her parents get up in the morning, do even one thing a day, let people support them through their grief, or have small expectations for a future?

As Annie's doctor, I take her hand. I let her cry. I hold her. I am standing in the circle supporting her, never having experienced her loss, hoping I never do. At my side are my own palpable fears about losing someone so close. As I learn just a little bit more about myself, I wonder how to practice that courage to put one foot in front of the other and then do it again.

Staying

Anonymous

Her husband is an alcoholic. She is a cancer survivor. She goes to Al-Anon and still lives with her husband. I marvel at that. She knows his alcoholism is his problem. She does not feel she is a silent enabler, allowing him to slowly kill himself, but rather that she is separating the person from the behavior. From what I can see, she is coping by accepting him where he is, taking care of herself, and sometimes expressing frustration to me and carefully selected others.

I can interpret this in many ways. Is this sheer dedication? Foolishness? Today, at least for today, I am looking at this as brave, a choice to live in the difficult space between black and white, and I appreciate the reminder that this space is real.

"How are the Boys?"
Sharon Dobie

She never fails to ask, "How are the boys?"

She comes in monthly, with her daughter and her walker. Dressed in her jeans, and T-shirt, her graying hair braided down her back, bulky sweater over her thin sixty-year-old-but-looks-older-than-that frame, she slowly makes her way from the waiting room to the exam room, sometimes in slippers and when her swelling is less, in shoes. We have known each other for more than twenty years, she and I, and we feel like old friends. Sometimes the familiarity between us worries me. In the routine of our monthly visits when I refill her pain medications, will my comfort result in missing a clue that something larger or more ominous needs attention? Do I solidly keep tuned to her needs and not let my sense of ease or her congeniality distract me from my job?

This patient has always been medically fragile. She has Marfan's syndrome, an odd genetic condition where one's connective tissues lack tensile strength. As a result, bones are not held stably in place at the joints. Dislocations and arthritis are givens. Vital tissues like heart valves and major blood vessels like the aorta lack strength and are prone to rupture. The lens in one of my patient's eyes has slid to the side, no longer held in place by the tissues meant to do the job.

Twenty years ago, every gynecologist I consulted agreed that my patient needed a hysterectomy, but worried that her tissues would not heal after surgery. It took many calls to many surgeons before I found one willing to operate. Now that her condition has not brought the early death that many had predicted, what is most important is her pain. No surgeon will operate on the hips, knees, and shoulders that rub, bone on bone, with her every movement. Her walker, an occasional ride in a wheel chair so her daughter can take her out, and her pain medication accompany her internal acceptance of what is.

We have shared stories over the years – the death of her husband, her teenaged children's pregnancies, and now her own failing health. She tells me she is up and dressed every day and sometimes, though less often now, cares for grandchildren while her daughter works. She and her daughter take in other young relatives when their parents are unable to care for them. She knows I cannot fix her joints or her family's emotional stressors. She knows there are real limits to how much I can even mitigate her pain. But though she hurts in more ways than one, she carries on.

Many of my patients inquire about my family and my life during our visits, and she is no exception: "How are the boys?" She has heard about their successes and our challenges, and has commiserated and laughed with me along the way. I wonder if she knows that drawing me back to my sons connects me to her story in a way that gives me strength. Her persistent presence in her children's lives, regardless of their issues or her health, sets a standard for me. Her tenacity to carry on keeps the bar raised high. I wonder if she sees it as the courage I see.

Chapter 4

A Good Death

Leaving is Not So Bad

Sharon Dobie

His breathing had become labored, and he was awake only a few minutes of every hour or two. His arms, legs, face, and stomach were swollen to twice their normal size from the edema. He reclined in a hospital bed in the living room of his tiny apartment, while his parents occupied his bedroom. The room was very warm because he often felt chilled. He knew he was dying and asked his parents to call me. Kaposi's sarcoma, an AIDS diagnosis, was a death sentence in the days before antiretroviral drugs. AIDS may now be a chronic instead of a terminal illness for many, but years ago, this was not the case. We all knew Stephen was likely to die from complications of AIDS.

When he was diagnosed, he was an anxious art student in his early twenties who had no idea what he wanted to do with his life. Stunned by his Kaposi's and AIDS diagnoses, he initially shut himself in his apartment except for his part-time job and medical appointments. "The world has stopped," he said. "I can't think or sleep."

In his early months with AIDS, part of our visits included talking about his fear of dying. He would tell me how terrified he was of possible pain and also of death. "I do NOT want to die. I'm too young to be thinking about being dead. What happens when you're dead anyway? Can't you find something that'll make me not die? I mean really, Sharon, I'm too young to be dead. Why do I have this curse, this going-to-die thing over my head every damn minute?"

As he talked, I could almost see his heart pumping harder and faster, keeping tempo with the mounting hysteria in his voice. My heart was keeping time with his; I didn't like thinking about his or anyone's death because then I would be thinking about my own. Usually I would remind my patient that he might survive me, that I could be hit by a car today, that both of us better take heed and live our lives the best we could. I don't know if it calmed or fooled him; it did not calm me. Since I had a close friend with Kaposi's, I worried about both Stephen and him, and everyone close to me, and I worried about me! I wanted no one around me to die, including me.

Before and after his AIDS diagnosis Stephen would tell hysterically funny jokes in the midst of his anxious explosions. A few months after his diagnosis of AIDS, he mustered his talents and chronicled his story in cartoons. To his surprise, they were published. The publicity drew him out. He became a standup comedian who performed locally, and he continued to draw cartoons depicting his life as "not just an AIDS patient." Thousands of people with AIDS and their families, friends, and caregivers saw and identified with his brutally honest humor.

I had not been Stephen's doctor for the last few years of his life because he preferred the atmosphere of the health center that I had left. We stayed in touch though, including through his participation on panels for medical students about living with AIDS. My friend with the Kaposi sarcoma died during that interval. Now a number of years later, there I was at his bedside and he was dying. I was there to say goodbye.

I remember his living room, the hospital bed in the center, with most of the other furniture pushed to the side, and I remember the shallow irregular breathing that heralds the end of a life. I told him how much I respected what he did with the years he lived with AIDS, and that I knew he was dying and appreciated his calling me to visit. He slept a lot.

There were also two brief exchanges. I was sitting, quietly reflecting on all that he had accomplished. How anxious he had been as a young man! Silently I marveled at how he had used his anxiety to hone his art, and how his artistic expression had seemed to calm and give voice to his anxiety, serving thousands of strangers, whether they had the disease, were close to someone with it, or were just angry about its devastation. Lost in those thoughts, I felt tears coming. Suddenly his eyes snapped open and he rolled his eyes. "I did not invite you here to cry!" he said. My response was just as quick, "You knew what you were getting when you picked me for your doctor!" "Oh yeah, that's for sure," he laughed and was asleep again.

A little while later, still sleeping, he smiled. He started to chuckle quietly.

This lasted several minutes and then he opened his eyes, got very quiet and smiled. "This is not so bad. It is not scary like I thought it would be." Those were the last words I heard from him.

Most of us will experience the deaths, perhaps premature and tragic, of some who are close to us. One person's death might exemplify the way we would like to die; another's might be traumatic for us. My mother died of cancer over months. My father dropped dead changing planes in Dallas. My grandmothers had complications of dementia, and my Grandfather stopped taking his meds, knowing that prostate cancer was invading his bones. And because of my work, like other health care providers, I may witness more deaths and work with more grieving families than those who are not in medicine.

Our patients' deaths can evoke many feelings. It can be deeply distressing because we are trained to prevent death. Even if we see death as a release from something we can't fix, we still grapple with a sense of our own inadequacy peppered with guilt. But something more complex can happen within us. You can put me squarely on the list of those who lack what it takes to amble towards death with grace and acceptance. Yet here was one of my most anxious patients nearing death, one who had talked openly of his terror of dying, saying, "This is not so bad"—with a smile and a chuckle, no less. Though I have no opinion about how people should die, Stephen reassured me.

His Way and Marmalade

Jessie Fudge

As a medical student at the Veteran's Hospital, or VA, I had very few patients and a lot of time to spend with them. One was a war veteran who loved to travel the country in his large truck. He would spend weeks at a time alone in the woods with his dogs and always looked a bit disheveled, in a nature-loving sort of way. His long wavy gray hair, weathered face, and well-worn pants and shoes made him the picture of a tough survivor, and he had the endless stories of animal, bear, and nature encounters that reinforced that image. As I listened to his stories with fear on my face, he would joke that it was much easier to survive a bear attack than a hospital stay.

He came to the VA emergency room with shortness of breath and an inability to walk his dogs as he used to. He had been very healthy otherwise, which may have been why he had rarely sought health care in the past. He was very surprised to be admitted to the hospital, and voiced his opposition on a daily basis.

"I don't want to be here. Why am I here? Can't you help me if I'm home?" Home was his truck out in the woods with his dogs and his solitude. He had a cabin, but he only went there to check his mail, pay bills, tend to the upkeep of the cabin, and to make marmalade.

I was his primary provider during his hospital stay, along with specialty teams involved in his care. He looked to me to translate their discussions and recommendations into terms he could understand. When he was finally diagnosed with terminal lung cancer, I wanted to be the one to tell him, but I had never presented news like this before. It was and still is the hardest conversation I have ever had. He listened quietly as I tried to weigh the recommendation of long chemotherapy courses in the hospital against his desire to return to his former life.

After the team left and only he and I were in the room, he had few questions. "When can I see my dogs? Will I live long enough to go on another trip into the woods? The woods are where I am most comfortable."

These were hard questions. The oncologists recommended chemotherapy and radiation treatment; no treatment was not one of their options. But the treatments were unlikely to cure him, and would not allow him to be away from the hospital for long periods of time. After every discussion with the oncologist, the patient would remind me, "You don't need to cure me. I'm not afraid. I just want to go on one more trip. I don't want to die in the hospital." He wanted to die his way.

In the end, we were able to arrange multiple three-day retreats away from the hospital between chemotherapy sessions. This gave him time to make it up to his cabin, but not all the way north to the woods. Although he was always extremely weak when he returned, he was glad to have gone and unhappy to be back.

In a final care conference, he made the decision that he wanted us to do all we could, not to treat the cancer, but to make him strong enough to return to the woods of northern Minnesota so he could die where he was most at home. Having no family, he sought my approval for his decision. I supported it even though it was a hard decision for me as a medical student and I knew it would be hard for many physicians to make. It sure was not something taught in a medical school classroom.

After several weeks of palliative treatment, meal replacement shakes, and physical therapy, he left the hospital to return to the woods. I struggled to balance the hopeless feeling that medicine had failed him with the joy that I had been able to truly listen to him and guide him in his final journey. After his discharge from the hospital, I received a jar of marmalade from him, along with a letter thanking me for caring. I never heard from him after that.

In treating this terminally ill patient, I realized that medicine is not always about curing a patient's illness and extending a life, but is about helping people find the strength to live a full life to the end. Now I approach patients as members of their care teams and never forget to ask each patient what the long-term treatment goal is.

This patient spurred many discussions as I contemplated how I would like to leave this world if I had the choice. He and I were very alike, and I think about him frequently as I navigate life's choices, trying to choose the path that lets me live my life to the fullest. The unopened jar of marmalade is still in my refrigerator, reminding me that I too would choose more happiness over more time.

We Don't Know When
Kelly Gabler

"I just don't know what I am going to do without her," her husband said to me through audible sobs as we talked on the phone that afternoon. I had come to know Mrs. H in a variety of settings: acute-care hospital stays, the long-term acute-stay facility, the skilled nursing facility, the clinic, and even a visit to her home, where a resident and I got lost as we drove into the country on its twisting roads.

She had been sick, really sick, for as long as I'd known her, a little over a year. Her end-stage congestive heart failure kept her on oxygen at home, and she had been hospitalized for this condition four times in the past year; she was even intubated on the most recent two admissions until we could get the extra fluid off her lungs with our powerful medicines and she could breathe on her own. When I saw her in the clinic I always knew the nurses were going to miss half their lunch break - just reconciling and clarifying what medicines she was taking from the last hospital stay would take 15 minutes. Then we would have to debate about benzodiazepines and narcotics as her anxiety and pain crippled her even more than her deteriorating lungs.

I always liked her, even though I was mentally and emotionally exhausted after every encounter. I would work hard to make her better, though knowing that what I was doing would have little impact on her long-term survival. I didn't mind missing lunch or staying late because I knew how important it was for her to have as much of my time as possible.

She was hurting; she was miserable. I knew her pain and anxiety added to the disability caused by her organic diseases. As a new physician I had seldom crossed the threshold of prescribing "controlled substances" - medications like narcotics and valium that are regulated because they might be abused and are addictive. Worrying that I might contribute to addiction, I was afraid to pull out my prescription pad and request these drugs for her. I went on to worry that my patient might die from taking medications that can cause respiratory depression. She would be dead and I would be hunted down by the medical board. But she was my path to appreciating how true a phrase can be: "Oxycodone allows her to function."

I began to understand her day-to-day struggles just to manage ordinary life activities. We tried to negotiate some regimen of less potent narcotics, but when I looked into her eyes I saw that she was still in pain, and that she was scared the pain would get worse, not better. As my relationship with her developed I came to trust her and to trust myself. I learned to imagine what it would be like to be in this person's shoes, just hoping to suffer less. I pulled out that controlled-substance prescription pad. We also discussed whether she would want to be intubated again. Resuscitation and hospice came up, too, but she could not bring herself to make a decision acknowledging that the end of her life might be near.

In the end I think my patient regained some small amount of control over her life and death when she made the choice to stay at home during her last episode of heart failure. When I learned that she died in her sleep after having breathing troubles but choosing not to go to the hospital, I felt mixed emotions: sad to lose her but relieved that her suffering was over. I called her husband and after we talked for more than half an hour I gave him my cell phone number, something I had never done before. Although he was not my patient, I wanted to be there for him as a kind of bereavement counselor, helping him to begin to process what he would do with the rest of his life.

In an ideal world we would all have the chance to say goodbye to those who have played an important role in our lives, but so often that does not happen. Talking with my patient's husband about her life helped me to tell her good bye. The experience reinforced my habit of telling my loved-ones that I love them as often as I can. Each encounter with a patient or a family member or friend might be my last, so I always want to make it special.

A Lady Always Knows
Sarah Hale

We'd been having a rough month on the Family Medicine Service - which had become more of a terminal cancer service. Ms. R was an otherwise pretty healthy 86-year old woman admitted for pneumonia that had not responded to outpatient treatment. Over the course of the next day or two, it became clear that she had advanced lung cancer. She took this news in stride and did not even seem surprised. Instead she started telling us about how wonderful her life had been, all the things that had been fulfilling to her—a wonderful marriage to her now very deaf husband, who hovered around her, tending to her in his very loud voice, her wonderful children and grandchildren, the amazing adventures she'd had. She agreed to further testing and treatment for the sake of her children, or at least agreed when they were in the room. Because of her reflections and comfort with her diagnosis, I believe that she knew she was dying when she came to the hospital even though her family was surprised.

Hospital teams often hold "family meetings" that include the patient, key family members, and the medical team, to discuss a patient's condition, the patient's goals for treatment, and the options the medical team can offer. At this patient's family meeting, she agreed with her daughter to remain "full code" and to schedule further testing. "Full code" means that if her heart stopped or she needed to receive electrical shocks or CPR to restart her heart, or if she needed to be intubated, we would be expected to proceed with these most aggressive therapies.

Once her family left for the evening, she asked to be changed to DNR, "Do Not Resuscitate," and to be kept comfortable with palliative care only. When asked if she was certain, Ms. R smiled and said, "A lady always knows when it's time to leave a party."

Ms. R's respiratory status decompensated quickly overnight. She became unresponsive. On rounds the next morning, I was at her bedside as her heart stopped beating. I've taken care of a number of patients who have died, and I have been called to the bedside of a patient who had just died. But this was the first (and still only) time I was present at the moment of death.

Physicians see so much illness and death that it can be numbing. We distance ourselves, build defensive walls, and use black humor because we fear that the grief and loss will be overwhelming. Towards the end of a sad month filled with loss, and watching many people struggle with end-of-life issues, Ms. R was so graceful, so at peace, satisfied, content, and ready for her life to end, that caring for her was healing to the staff. As her provider, I felt like she wanted to comfort me about her approaching death. In addition to healing me during a month of loss, Ms. R gave me an aspiration—to live my life in such a way that I can also accept death and, when my time comes, leave the party gracefully.

Thank you, to a gracious lady.

Detox Redemption

Anonymous

It was the end of my first year as a Family Medicine resident, and my fellow interns and I were tired. It's no excuse, but when we're weary we can characterize and generalize patients too readily.

"He collapsed on the way home from the bar. Multiple pulmonary emboli, probably some sort of a lung cancer in there, though the radiologists say it's hard to tell with the pneumonia and edema. He's stable though. Starting warfarin and all for the blood clots. I haven't had a chance to check on him since the admission; could you just go see how he's doing if you get a chance?" That was sign-out as my ICU partner hurried off to clinic, and I grudgingly trudged to the chart rack to write notes as a way to put off having to tell someone I had never met that he very likely had cancer.

While not explicitly stated, the distilled version of the intensive care unit (ICU) sign-out made clear that Mr. Bright, unlike his name, was an alcoholic. When I did go and talk with him, it turned out Mr. Bright described himself pretty much the same way.

His room was sunny and ultra-modern. The cardiac intensive care unit, or CCU, was the newest part of our hospital, with private, glass-enclosed rooms like the hospitals you see on TV. A heavy-set but strong-looking man with close-cropped white hair sat in the Geri-chair with his eyes closed, the sun beaming in on his face. The oxygen tube in his nostrils was upside-down.

"Mr. Bright?" I asked, hesitantly. He opened his eyes, completely awake. I introduced myself, sitting on the end of the bed to indicate I had come to chat for a while. "How are you feeling?" I asked, dutifully. He paused for a few breaths before answering. "Pretty crappy, but I guess better than yesterday."

"Could you tell me again what happened?" I asked.

"Well, I shouldn't have gone. I knew that, really. Haven't been able to get out of bed for a while without feeling bad," he continued, slowly. "Been getting so dizzy, and I'm so weak. Can't breathe after a few steps." He paused again, and I waited. Silence seemed a natural part of his speech, making it not as uncomfortable as usual. "I guess I just figured, what difference would drinking a beer make if I'm this sick anyway? Been killing myself my whole life, really. This time, pretty much all I had to do was go to the bar or to the liquor store. I knew I wasn't going to make it back.

"I just sat down on the sidewalk. I couldn't breathe, couldn't see straight even though I wasn't drunk, not even close. Sat there probably an hour. Surprised I didn't just die there, I guess. Then this stranger shows up and asks if I'm ok. Not sure what I said to him, but maybe it didn't make sense because he must have called 9-1-1." Mr. Bright almost chuckled for a second, but then the moment passed and he frowned again but didn't go on.

I finally broke the silence. "What did they tell you about why you were admitted here, about what's happened to your lungs?" His eyes were closed again.

"Blood clots. Pneumonia." He replied.

Clearly no one had mentioned cancer. I waited a moment and then confirmed his understanding. "Did they talk about how difficult it is to see all the parts of your lungs because of the pneumonia?" He opened his eyes in silent questioning. I hesitated, wondering not for the first or last time, whether it was wise or foolish to warn someone of an extremely likely but unconfirmed diagnosis. Studying Mr. Bright's face for a moment I decided, more by gut than by logical deduction, that he would be angry to discover he hadn't been told the whole truth at the start.

I explained to him that there was a lot of fluid in his lungs, so if there were other problems underneath the pneumonia it would be hard to see until the infection cleared up and the blood clots dissolved a bit. "That may be all that's there," I admitted. "But when we see so many blood clots, there's usually a reason, and I just want to warn you ahead of time that the most common cause of clots like this is having a cancer somewhere." After he didn't respond, I started to doubt the wisdom of having told him, and rushed to clarify that I was not diagnosing him but just wanted to be clear that we would be looking for any source of cancer as he recovered.

I waited what seemed like five minutes.

"Well, it wouldn't really be a surprise, would it?" he finally replied, rocking slightly in the chair and looking out the window.

"I think it's always a shock," was the only thing I could think of to say. Critical Care Unit duty makes doctors and nurses experience the difficult

ramifications of the denial of death. We push futile treatments on the terminally ill or elderly, aggressively playing God without regard to suffering,
in absurd choices we would never even impose on our pets. But intensive
care is also the place you realize how much that same denial protects us vulnerable human beings. Without it, we would never take a risk, never cross
the street or ride in an airplane or give our hearts to others. So it is, in fact,
a complicated emotional experience to sit there in the room with death's
presence.

"Do you have family?" I asked. Mr. Bright did – an eldest son from a
first wife, long since "lost to follow-up," much like we refer to a patient who
does not return for care. Two daughters, one from the second wife and one
from the third, were around. They would talk to their father if he called, but
that was about it. He was living with his youngest child, a son who needed
rent money more than he needed or wanted a father. So Mr. Bright handed
over to the son most of the disability check he got each month for an old
back injury from his construction job days. He said that we should call his
son, keep him in the loop. I nodded. He closed his eyes and turned toward
the sun again, signaling the end of that afternoon's conversation.

As the days went on and the infection and blood clots cleared, the inevitable lung cancer couldn't evade exposure. Each day new masses peeked
out through a more translucent chest x-ray. Mr. Bright was transferred to a
regular room and then put on nursing home status. There were no nursing
home beds that accepted him in our community, so he languished on our
hospital service for days, then weeks, then months.

I had finished my month in the ICU and three weeks doing dermatol-
ogy when I returned to a rotation on the medicine inpatient service, saw
Mr. Bright's name on the patient roster, and strolled back into his room. I
was surprised to find a visitor, a blond woman in her early forties with dark-
rimmed glasses and a warm smile. I introduced myself to Mr. Bright, not
expecting him to remember me.

"Oh, I remember," he sounded like he would have laughed if not for
discomfort. "You told me about the cancer. Bet you didn't expect to find me
still here after so long."

"Well, I thought you would survive the ICU," I replied, "but have to
admit I don't know many people who have survived hospital food for six
weeks."

"Well, it's healthier than beer," he quipped. "This is my daughter," he said, gesturing toward the visitor. "Not sure how she found me, but turns out she and her family live a few towns away." At this point he sighed; I couldn't tell if it was from relief or guilt. "Turns out I have a granddaughter, too; still hoping to meet her." The daughter explained that she had married late and after several years of trying, gave birth to a daughter, now six months old. Mr. Bright had missed all of his daughter's experiences; they had never been close, and her engagement had come about during the time when his drinking was out of control. She had had enough of him, but then there was that word: cancer. She could not just leave him alone to die, so when her brother called, she came. Now, on her third visit, she was growing more comfortable with her father, but still hadn't brought her husband and daughter along.

When my attending physician arrived, we attempted to examine Mr. Bright, but found that he couldn't get out of his chair without severe pain. While in that Never Neverland of being a nursing home patient with no nursing home available, residing in an acute care hospital means having reduced care. No one had really noticed the gradual onset of his weakness and growing discomfort. He had staked his whole reputation on his toughness and was not about to tell anyone how much he hurt or how he really felt.

We ordered X-rays and found metastatic cancer lesions throughout his skeleton. We increased his pain medication and arranged for radiation therapy to stabilize the bone, but it was clear that time was not on Mr. Bright's side. Each day it was more difficult for him to tolerate an exam, to get out of bed, to maintain his positive take on his troubles.

But he clearly cherished every moment with his rediscovered family. The metastasis of the cancer convinced the daughter to overcome her reluctance to trust a father who had always disappointed her, and she brought her family to meet him. Mr. Bright cheered up amid the unquestioning love of a six-month-old and her attention to her grandfather.

He continued in our hospital service, now much too ill for a nursing home to accept him. On a Friday afternoon in early spring, near the end of my three weeks on the hospital service, I found his daughter's family, even his son, gathered in his room. It had been a bad day for Mr. Bright in which he had barely been able to communicate with them, and now he was sleeping fitfully under the effects of his pain medication. I had just come to check on him before I left for the weekend, so I chatted with them for a few moments. And then it occurred to me that this cancer was so obscure to them, hidden within a man who had been a stranger on so many levels.

"Do you want to see it?" I asked. In a way that physicians and patients rarely achieve, we were all speaking the same language for the moment; they knew I was referring to the cancer. The daughter, as the implicitly elected leader, nodded solemnly. Her husband picked up the baby and all four followed me down the hall.

The hospital's lawyer would have been aghast if she had heard of this field trip, I realized later. Without Mr. Bright's permission, I was opening a part of his medical record to his family. And I was taking "civilians" into a part of the hospital where they were forbidden for security and privacy reasons. Neither of those issues occurred to me at the time. Mr. Bright himself seemed to be a part of our intuitive conversation that day, and I felt no doubt that he would approve. I had also bypassed a few hallway computer terminals and taken the family straight to the viewing station in the radiology suite, which I knew would be abandoned this late on a Friday afternoon.

We gathered silently in the sacred dusk of the radiologists' lair, and I opened his CT scan images to reveal the large cancer and fluid taking up most of his left lung and several spots of his right lung. The picture made it obvious that he was breathing with less than a quarter of his natural lung capacity. The daughter and son-in-law both gasped. I had done the same when I had first seen the image, shocked at the rapid growth of malignant tissue since his admission barely two months before.

The daughter finally broke the silence. "How long has he had it?"

"I can't say for sure," I admitted. "It's certainly grown very aggressively in the last few months. But lung cancer is usually present for a number of years before it becomes obvious, sometimes just a year or two, sometimes ten. It's really hard to know."

"Oh my God," she replied. "All that drinking..." her voice trailed off. That was it. We said nothing more, but a tension that had lived among all of us those last months was suddenly gone, as if it had been exhaled by that last little bit of healthy lung.

We parted ways in the hall as they made their way back to his bedside and I headed to my car for the commute home. Although I received a call and a note from the daughter, I would never see them again in person. It was no surprise when Mr. Bright died the following Sunday. His family was at his side.

I had witnessed a medical miracle. It wasn't a cure for cancer or even a relieving of pain, but rather something more difficult to achieve: forgiveness. I am not a surgeon, or an emergency room physician or a cancer specialist. I will probably never cure or save anyone. But just being there means sometimes you are part of those moments that make you believe in people and our ability to take care of one another, even when we don't get it right the first time. It is both humbling and empowering to realize that a self-described "drunk" reminded me of the importance of forgiveness. Too often I don't get things right at first, and sometimes never do, but I still feel the healing at those times when I am able to forgive myself.

The Fairway and the Grand Piano; Dying With Grace in the Era of Fighting to Live

Hank Pelto

I'm trained to make people live. Live forever, really, is the undercurrent of the medical field and graduate medical education. Extend the cardiopulmonary life of a patient with terminal cancer by two months for $100,000? You bet! Write the order and sign the check! But, the question we all ask at some point is, "Is this really living?" During my second year of residency I was deeply struggling with this question. Fresh from multiple experiences with families trying to let go, patients grappling with what to do next and defaulting to "everything," and a personal life experience with my father-in-law desperately seeking permission to give up, I met two men—let's call them the Fairway and the Grand Piano.

The Fairway was a man in his 70s I met "on call" one day at the VA hospital. He was a scheduled admission, and all I knew about him initially was that he had recently been diagnosed with lung cancer. In the VA admission rat race this was often all I really "needed" to know. I would do the admission paperwork and write a diet order, someone I never spoke with would give him chemotherapy, and several days later I would discharge him. This time was unexpectedly different.

A quick glance at the notes told me this lifelong smoker reluctantly came for evaluation when he could no longer walk a block without getting short of breath. His chest x-ray looked like a ball pit, where children play in a sea of plastic balls. His hospital room was a favorite of mine, looking out over Jefferson Golf Course in Seattle. When I walked into this room I always took a moment to look out the window and reflect how much I wished I were out on the course. This day was no different. But the patient was also looking intently at the golf course. We moved quickly through his symptoms, my exam, and the plan because he had had similar conversations many times before.

We finally got to simply chatting. He was a Vietnam vet with grown children he wasn't very close to. He had long struggled with PTSD and was a retired lineman. In his retirement he moved to North Bend and got a job for a few bucks an hour mowing the greens at the local golf course. Two perks he loved about the job were that he could play as much as he wanted for free and he could mow whenever he wanted. The latter came in particularly handy. When he would wake from yet another flashback nightmare in the wee hours of the morning, the fairway was always there, ready to be mowed. He had never found anything that soothed him as well as mowing did.

He was clear with me that he only came into the hospital for information. He wanted to know what was going on so that he could move on. "I know what this means," he told me. "What's really important to me is that I am cremated and that my ashes are spread on the fourth fairway." I wondered, would he finally be at peace there?

The first thing the Grand Piano asked me when I walked into his room was "Did you listen to my music?" A little taken aback, I stammered that I had not. "Oh, OK, a lot of people have been coming in and saying they listen to my music on my website." He was a musician, classical, and had traveled the world, playing and teaching. His passion was palpable when he talked about his music and his life. During a trip to Thailand to visit his partner he had started having abdominal pain. He waited until he got home several weeks later to get checked out. Then he waited a little longer, certain that it would go away. Having no insurance, he wanted to make sure it was serious. It did not get better, and finally he came to the VA to get checked out.

His labs looked OK, but his symptoms had worsened and his belly was swelling. The CT showed a liver with an assortment of gold nuggets and tennis balls lodged inside. Like Fairway, he was here for information. I met him several days into his workup, and the word "terminal" had mostly sunk into his psyche. As we waited for loved ones to arrive from distant lands for the family meeting, he made one thing clear to me: he wanted to sit at his grand piano, and soon.

Death is tough. It is individual. People have to do it themselves. Some embrace it quickly, others slowly. Others fight it to the last breath. The Fairway and the Grand Piano helped me remember that option 1 is available, and that my medical-schooled reflex toward option 3 is not the only way. These men helped me grow more than they would ever realize.

The Birthday Party
Sharon Dobie

Finding meaning from some deaths is hard. With pagers ringing on a busy service, pulling the team to the needs of many patients, it was a challenge to slow down enough to comprehend even one of the layers of feelings evoked when I was working with a dying child. Jason was a very thin and very ill, still-handsome 11-year-old kid. His bone cancer had returned, and he was in the hospital for terminal care in the days before hospice was as available as it is now. He knew he was dying. His parents and younger brother were there most of the time, sometimes watching TV or reading quietly if he was sleeping. When he was awake, his pain was well controlled and he lay listless in his bed, seeming smaller by the day. Looking at him, we wondered, "How is he still alive? What does he need?" We felt inadequate to figure out what was keeping him alive, while at the same time, we felt a pull to keep him alive to stave off what we feared would be his family's horror and grief at his death. We felt helpless and sad.

One day after rounds, we noticed his family had gone out for a while. A couple of us went in to visit with him. We were talking about sports and school and whatever was on TV and we asked him, "If you were to make a list of things you want to do and things that worry you, what would they be?" His response was immediate: "I am really afraid I am going to wreck my brother's birthday." "What do you mean?" was our puzzled reply. "If I die before his birthday, my family won't have his party and his birthday will be wrecked." We tried to reassure him without negating his fears and left that conversation unsettled.

After we recovered somewhat and huddled, we returned to his bedside with a suggestion. How about we ask his parents to celebrate the birthday ahead of time? His face brightened as he talked about red balloons, noisemakers, and chocolate cake for his little brother.

It was an event attended by his brother, their parents, and other family members, all in his hospital room. There were laughter and red balloons, chocolate cake and ice cream that day. There was a calm in his face and his family after that and he died a few days later. None of us young doctors were parents yet, and we knew we could barely grasp his family's grief. We were all fairly stunned that he died so quickly after the party, but I was left with his lesson for me. He had cut away the unnecessary and the less necessary to identify and choose the focus of his last attention.

Heeding the Spirits
Sharon Dobie

In lu-Mien culture, if you want the spirit of the dying person to find rest after their death, you cannot discuss death with them. Unrest is the last thing we wanted for Mrs. N, a 92-year old matriarch. Her people, the Yao from China, had migrated to Laos prior to her birth. When the Laotians targeted the lu-Mien, who were believed to be aiding and abetting the Americans, many lu-Mien fled Laos. In her 60s, Mrs. N escaped on foot from Laos, her home country, with her husband, adult children, and their spouses and children, all carrying their possessions. They found their way first to a refugee camp in Thailand, and then to Seattle, where they had made their life since the early 1980s.

The surgeons, the oncologists, and I had known of her cancer for more than ten years, but Mrs. N had refused surgery and other treatment. Several times, with the assistance of interpreters and lu-Mien elders, we discussed her condition and our recommendations. We had her meet with a mental health professional to be sure she was both competent and not depressed. She chose no intervention, and we lived with her choice. Now she was dying.

As she neared death, on hospice at home, I went to visit her. Her first words to me were, "I want an operation now. I have too much pain." My stomach hit the floor. She had refused surgery when it would have been possible and helpful. Now it would be neither.

I was searching for a response, when her sons reminded me, "Her sister had surgery and she died during the operation." They did not need to say more. Behind her words was the unspoken wish for an operation that would hasten her death. I reassured her that we had many options to help with the pain. She seemed to relax a bit. Her sons, their wives and her husband were there. We all knew we could not speak of dying. Instead, during the next hour, her children told stories. They talked of their early years in Laos, helping farm the hillside, their mother always out in the field with them. Even then, their stories said, she had seemed more in charge than her younger husband, their father. They retold the tale of their walk hundreds of miles from their village. Driven out by the war, they slept at a distance from the road, found food and water, and when they were running out of both, Ms. N fed the children first. When they finally reached a refugee camp, they were weak and malnourished. The children thanked their mother for teaching them, never leaving them, loving them. The room quieted with the stories, and there were only three audible sounds: their voices weaving their family story, the interpreter speaking quietly to the hospice social worker and me, and Mrs. N's breathing. She visibly relaxed when they began reassuring her with their plans for their lives in the future. Drifting into a peaceful sleep, she died a few days later without a recurrence of the anxiety that had been present at the start of that visit.

There are many ways to say good-bye.

Chapter 5

Unexpected Hope

This chapter is dedicated to one of the contributors, Doctor Mitchell L. Cohen MD. Mitch was a rural family medicine doctor who practiced in a small community in southwestern Washington. He died suddenly in 2010 at 39, leaving his wife, three young children, and a grieving community of patients who counted on him. I never met Mitch despite having hoped to. He was the only person who responded to a request for narratives that I posted in our Washington Academy of Family Physicians newsletter several years before his death. The story he sent follows. In the weeks before his death, we communicated by email. He edited his story and sent it back to me with a promise to write and send me more narratives for this collection. While he could not keep that promise, I am pleased his family consented to his contribution staying in this project.

The Christmas Gift
Mitchell Cohen

Working long hours during medical school in Chicago and even longer ones during a family medicine residency in the Pacific Northwest, I found myself drawing blood from patients handcuffed to their gurneys, being spit on by the intoxicated, being conned by drug seekers, and taking histories from gang members who invariably claimed "I was just minding my own business, when someone shot me." Teaching hospitals can be places of misery and suffering for both the patients and the students of medicine. This was not why I wanted to be a doctor.

Skepticism and cynicism were the cultural norms during my professional indoctrination. In the medical education hierarchy, physicians near the top subtly, or not so subtly, redirected unwanted cases to where I lived: at the bottom. A senior resident once told me, "all shit flows downhill," and by the time I was a senior resident I found myself passing patients down along with the same proverbial wisdom. "A good teaching case" or "a wonderful educational opportunity" was code for, "Here, 'tern, you deal with this."

With the hope of escape after residency, I took a job as a physician in a small logging and farming town. My schedule quickly filled, but along with folks you'd expect from quaint small-town America – shopkeepers, farmers, school kids, retired loggers – there were also patients with the same psychosocial dysfunctions as in the cities. I wondered, "Was it the health care system that brought this out, the human condition, or just a black cloud surrounding me?" I was thirty-three, at the beginning of my career, thousands of dollars in debt, and part of me didn't know how long I could stay in patient care.

Filled with pessimism and near desperation, on a hot summer day in the middle of August I met Molly, midway through her pregnancy. She had been seen by an obstetrician in the area, but said, "We did not get along, so I came to you." Admitting to past methamphetamine abuse, which she attributed to underlying depression, she claimed she was clean. I was skeptical, and interpreted her not getting along with her prior obstetrician as "He fired me when I wouldn't stop using drugs." She did admit she used tobacco, but like many smokers she was supposedly trying to cut back. The father of the baby wasn't involved. Going through the motions, I gave her my canned talk on the outpatient management of pregnancies. She agreed to come back in two weeks. At best I figured I had 50:50 chance of ever seeing Molly again.

To my surprise, two weeks later she returned. This time, instead of just reading the chart in front of me and examining the dust bunnies in the corner, I looked at her and saw she was not the bad toothed, picked-at skin gaunt figure whom I had already stereotyped her to be, but a curly haired blond young woman with smooth complexion and an engaging smile, in her mid-twenties. Her pregnancy was just beginning to show. As we talked, Molly asked out of the blue if I would run a urine drug test on her. Startled, I again jumped to conclusions.

"Is this a parole requirement?" I asked.

"No." she said, "I am going to put my baby up for adoption, and I need to show I am clean." Never taking her eyes off mine, she proceeded to lay out her plans. She was working with an adoption agency and had begun the process of considering families. "I'm going to stay clean for the baby's sake. Well, and mine, too," she concluded.

As Molly's pregnancy progressed, it was most notable for being uneventful. There were no weekly dramas or crises. There were no gaps in her care where staff were left wondering if she had slipped back into drug use. To avoid her heroin-using and abusive ex-boyfriend, she moved in with her mother, where she knew she would be safer and encouraged to make responsible decisions. She was taking care of herself, and in doing so, taking care of her baby the way a mother should. She quickly became one of my favorite patients, someone I enjoyed seeing on my schedule of patients for the day.

Despite this bond we were forming, I remained guarded and skeptical. I still couldn't let myself believe her self-discipline could last through her pregnancy. People, particularly methamphetamine addicts, don't easily change, and I had been lied to, stolen from, and cheated by people seemingly in recovery. "It's only a matter of time," I told myself. At every visit, I would look for clues that she was in trouble, unable to accept the goodness that was right in front of me. Molly was always dressed in clean, attractive clothes and was polite and compliant with her medical treatment, but I could not take these things at face value. At one point, to help explain the disconnect between her current appearance and demeanor and what I knew of her past, I almost convinced myself that she had been involved in prostitution and perhaps still was.

My other fear was that Molly would decide to raise the baby on her own instead of proceeding with the adoption plan. I had seen this before, too; a young woman initially shocked at the thought of childbirth and motherhood can warm to the idea as pregnancy progresses. Fantasy turns into full-blown magical thinking, and the story becomes: The father of the baby will come around, and we will be a happy family. My fear was that when this happy ending didn't materialize, she and her child would fall deeper into poverty, depression, and hopelessness.

None of this happened. Molly held to her original plans for giving up the baby. She came to every appointment and never had any signs of drug use, even in her urine toxicology screenings for illicit substances. She even quit smoking. At each visit she asked good questions about childbirth. She preferred not to talk about her past, and I respected that. I wanted to think of her as the mature woman in front of me and not as a meth addict or possible prostitute.

The week before Christmas, I received a phone call from Labor and Delivery. Molly was in labor. That evening she gave birth to a beautiful baby boy as healthy as any I've delivered. She notified the adoptive parents in Chicago (coincidentally the city where my medical career and cynicism began). A solid middle-class couple in their mid-thirties, they had been unsuccessful in conceiving. They caught the first available flight and arrived soon after delivery. Molly still had time to reconsider. I had seen birth moms hold their babies for the first time and, despite being no more prepared for motherhood than the day before, decide they could make it work. Molly spent time with the couple and never wavered. Everyone held the baby, and Molly seemed happy with this gift of her baby into the Chicago couple's lives.

In my post-partum visit with her in the hospital, she told me she knew this was the right decision for her. "It's not my time to be a parent; I am not ready. And it is their time to have a family." She was reassuring us both. On Christmas Eve, the new family boarded a plane to Chicago with the best Christmas present they ever could receive.

Patients have trust issues, but we doctors trump them. The medical education process all too often creates physicians who erect walls around themselves, leaving them detached and cold, cynical and jaded. Well, at least that is the effect my schooling had on me, and it carried over into my personal life. My detachment affected the way I viewed the world around me, from what I saw on the nightly news to the lives of my friends and neighbors. That Christmas will always stick in my mind as the year some of my walls started to come down. The negativism so ingrained in me lessened. Not everyone would reproduce Molly's achievements, but some could, and I was just a bit better at seeing more clearly the positive in each person, even the downtrodden, the depressed, and the addicted. There was room for generosity. That Christmas Molly gave me the gift of hope that there were others like her waiting to walk through my door.

Don't Give Up

Keisa Fallin-Bennett

Jack, a young man in his thirties, was a lifelong alcoholic. I met him in the ICU at a point where he had almost no potassium or phosphorus in his body, leaving him literally too weak to have the symptoms of alcohol withdrawal. He should have had tremors, at best, and probably seizures, but his muscles would have needed those two chemicals in his blood to show such signs of withdrawal. His alcohol use had also led to pancreatitis, an inflammation where the enzymes made by the pancreas to help digest food turn on the pancreas itself, destroying tissue and sometimes causing irreversible damage or even death.

Most of that month, late in my second year of residency, I felt like I presided only over his physical body, working to replenish and restore what was missing in his bloodstream, and giving him nutrition through his veins while his pancreas rested and hopefully healed. Then, after the chemicals were realigned, the withdrawal was over, and the pancreatitis was treated, I met the human being within, a very ill man who seemed to comprehend his situation.

In the last week of both his hospital stay and my inpatient rotation, his wife, family, and friends came to discuss their role in his treatment. What kind of rehabilitation was he willing to do? How well did he understand his addiction? He left the hospital the same day I did, with a less than perfect recovery plan. Our relationship continued because he became a patient in my outpatient clinic.

Over the next year Jack rarely showed up at the clinic, but called regularly with updates and requests for refills of his medications. He did not stop drinking. Though he did cut down, he was admitted twice more: alcohol withdrawal, hepatitis, pancreatitis. He challenged me by requesting outpatient detox treatment, but I was uncomfortable with that plan. Though I trusted his honesty, I didn't trust the alcoholic in him. He needed inpatient treatment. I researched, thought, discussed, and finally found some options to offer him. And I had to explain that I could not eliminate some large barriers: he was completely broke, had run out of severance and unemployment insurance pay, and had exhausted all varieties of insurance. That reduced the options to a very few. I told him how frustrated I was that the very people with the most potential to return to society and contribute could not get out of the hole that both they themselves and the health care system had been digging for decades.

Probably less than a month after that conversation, I was working a shift in the ER when a colleague cornered me to say Jack was again being admitted to the inpatient service. He had asked for me, and the resident requested that I stop in to say hello. It only took a glimpse into the room to see that the prognosis had changed from bad to dire. Jack laid there, bright yellow, practicing his early Kussmaul heaving breaths[2], his abdomen swollen with ascites.[3] He had stopped drinking three weeks before this. He had no money and had been feeling deeply tired. I was angry, but this time it was just with nature. Three months before, at his latest discharge, there had been no sign of liver failure. I had reassured him that with alcohol abstinence he still had a good chance. My medical training had not warned me that deterioration could happen this fast.

Jack survived the admission and acquired a liver specialist, but could not afford to see him. He applied for disability, and our state-funded Medicaid program provided some medications. He came back two weeks after that admission for another paracentesis, where we inserted a needle into the abdominal cavity to withdraw fluid. Overall he looked better. I tried to give him and his wife hope and even contacted the state's liver transplant hospitals to check on criteria. He now had almost two months of the six months of sobriety he needed to be put on the transplant list. I was about to graduate, and I worked with one of the interns to transfer his care to her after I left.

The week before graduation, I received a voicemail from his wife. The Friday before, he had begun to vomit blood, and she had taken him to a hospital closer to their home. When the liver is failing a person can develop vessels on the surface of the esophagus called varices, which are under very high pressure and at risk for rupturing and bleeding at all times. The doctors

---

2   Abnormally deep, very rapid sighing respirations characteristic of acidosis, a
      metabolic disorder.

3   Ascites is an abnormal collection of fluid in the abdominal cavity.

had done what they could, but the variceal floodgates were open too wide. He died. I heard his wife's shaky voice thanking me for my help and care, and then the lonely beep ending the call. Though I tried to contact her to learn the funeral arrangements, I never heard from her again.

The thing I most wanted to tell her —the thing that's hard to get across on a one-minute phone message— wasn't that I was terribly sorry for Jack. His suffering might have been worse had he lived. I was very sorry for her loss, and for the hope and longing cut off with his death, and I told her that in the voicemail. Mainly, though, I wanted to thank her, to thank him, for not giving up on me. I never gave up on Jack, because as a doctor I just treat people where they are. Doctors shouldn't give up on their patients; we should journey with them. The other direction, however, is crucial. Patients often give up on their doctors, many times with good reason. Jack had spent the last year of his life trusting me even when I didn't understand, even when I wasn't equipped to make expedited decisions about his treatment, even when I couldn't "do" or "fix" anything. I wanted to tell his wife that patients like Jack, who never gave up on me, are the ones who give young doctors hope in themselves.

Jazz, the Couch, and Video Games
Sharon Dobie

"We have an admission in the ER," began the resident on our inpatient service. "He is a man in his 20s, chronically disabled, with multiple congenital anomalies, including a uterostomy[4] and now with a urinary tract infection. He could probably go home, but he is vomiting and cannot keep anything down."

Further information revealed that he had several of these infections in recent months, and typically he needed a day or two of intravenous antibiotics before he could stop vomiting, eat, and go home on oral antibiotics. His anatomy, genetically distinctive and then altered with a tube draining urine from his abdomen, left him vulnerable to such infections. When I heard about his multiple abdominal and pelvic surgeries and his mobility challenges, I wondered what his life could be like.

I was remembering another young man who we had just recently discharged from the hospital. He was about the same age as our patient in the Emergency Room and he had chronic heart and lung disease. He lived at home with his parents, had finished high school, and that is where progress stopped for him. Or so it seemed to me. He didn't work and he wasn't in school. "I can't do much because of my condition," was his no smile or eye contact response to my question about whether he had a job.

When we admitted him, I had asked as I usually do, "How do you spend your days?" I was curious, imagining the long hours while his parents and buddies worked.

"Oh," he said, with a long sigh, a little sideways glance my way, but no change in tone, no smile, "I just play my video games."

"Do you go on the computer, network, look things up, watch movies, read?" I asked, searching not as much for content as for variety.

"No, I get my breakfast, take it to the couch, and play. That's kind of it. Sometimes a friend comes over and we play together. I don't go out or

---

4   A connection of the urinary bladder to the abdominal wall rather than to the urethra.

anything. I mean what would I do if I went out? I can't work or anything. It's ok, man."

The couch and video games: that was his life. We chatted while he was in the hospital about things he could do, the creation of a social network, and how vocational rehabilitation could work with him to find educational and training options leading to work. Well, I chatted. He did not seem very interested.

With that recent experience, what was I expecting when I went to the ER to see this new patient we were admitting for treatment of his urinary tract infection? I entered the emergency room both wondering and trying to hold back my assumptions. What did I expect him to say when I asked him how his life was? I did not have an answer in mind, but since I was surprised by his answers, I was probably half-expecting ones that underestimated who he is.

He was on his side on his emergency room gurney, an arm curled around a bag for vomiting . His mother was there, and the room was dark and quiet except when he moved and moaned. I introduced myself and asked his permission to ask him about his medical history and to examine him. Watching him and his discomfort, I again wondered what his life was like.

As he lay there in pain, nauseated and vomiting, he told me about college and his pursuits. He is a jazz pianist who had played with high school and college groups winning national awards, now with a jazz ensemble playing at local clubs, teaching piano, and working part time in a bookstore.

He was in a hospital, with serious medical challenges requiring intravenous antibiotics and medications to control his nausea. Yet that is not what defined him.

With our video-playing patient, I had felt saddened by what seemed like his overly constrained resignation to his limitation. Knowing that these two men face challenges I have never had to face, I still wondered what it takes for each of us to get to the place where acceptance doesn't limit us and where we still have the drive to overcome factors that might otherwise limit our choices. Discharging the video-game-playing young man, I really wondered how, in his place, I would handle his challenges. Then along came the young jazz pianist who showed me that special quality where his eyes were wide open to the cards he was dealt, and yet he was crafting an expressive, full, and socially connected life. I still don't know how I would respond if my life had circumstances like his. Yet he gave me hope.

Grabbing Time
Sharon Dobie

Hope does not have to mean a cure. When we hope, we believe some-thing positive is possible and we see a path towards it. "Never take away hope," physicians are taught, "even when delivering bad news." How often do I follow this teaching in my life? Do I see hope in the simple acts of our patients or of their loved ones living their lives? Do I acknowledge it? Does its apparent absence at times drain me professionally, or even personally?

I recall fourteen years ago like it was yesterday. My friend Meredith was coughing. She had allergies, she told me, and her nasal voice, throat clear-ing, and nose blowing supported that belief. She was also really close to being ten years out from her diagnosis and treatment of breast cancer. Two more months and some of us were going to throw her a party. Ten years! When the cough did not go away after the scratchy throat and runny nose responded to antihistamines, her doctor ordered a chest X-Ray.

She called me saying, "got some shitty news." The X-Ray showed what looked like a pleural effusion, a collection of fluid in the sac around the lungs.

"Well," I drew in a deep breath.

"They want to stick in a needle and take off some of the fluid to see what it is."

I sucked in more air. "Mer, that's good. Most often it's from an infec-tion; maybe instead of allergies you really had a little pneumonia and this is what is left."

I was hoping to convince her; I was hoping to convince me.

"Right." And then, "Will you come with me?"

"Of course."

About ten days later, we were sitting in the slightly cushioned straight-backed chairs of the waiting room for pulmonary procedures, staring at *Sports Illustrated* and *Sunset*, both of us wishing we could sink down in a comfortable easy chair with something better to take our minds off the next hour and Meredith's thoracentesis.

In this procedure, the goal is to place the needle at a level that will drain off enough fluid, but not so low as to be in danger of hitting one of the vital abdominal organs that hug right up under the diaphragm. To determine where to insert the needle and define how high up in the lung the fluid is located, the team first uses X-Ray, tapping on the back, and sometimes ultrasound. Then the patient leans forward, often over a table like the bedside tray tables in the hospital, hugging a pillow, and stays very still. The doctors mark the spot, usually in the middle of one side of the back, wash the area with an antiseptic solution, put a drape over the area, and inject local anesthetic in the skin and then down over the top of a rib and along the track that the larger needle will pass. Removing the anesthetic needle, they will then pass the larger needle through the skin and into the tissue. It is attached to a syringe and a valve connected to tubing. They continue inserting the needle slowly, touching the top of a rib as a reference point. Sticking bone hurts. As they pass over the rib, they slowly advance until they see that they are drawing fluid. Then the tubing is secured, in a variety of ways, depending on the particular setup and manufacturer. The patient meanwhile continues to sit, immobile, as no one wants a punctured lung, for as long as it takes to drain the fluid. That might be for only a minute or two if all that is wanted is 100 cc for some diagnostic reason. More often the aim is to siphon off up to two liters, to have enough to test for diseases and also to relieve the shortness of breath caused by the fluid collection compressing the lung and preventing it from expanding fully on inhalation.

Meredith was ready. Her doctor had reviewed the whole procedure with her and she had her questions answered. She was a get-it-over-and-done-and-let's-move-on kind of woman. The team performing Meredith's procedure led her off to their procedure room, leaving me pacing the waiting room. Forty minutes later she walked out, looked me in the eye, and said the line I dreaded: "Let's get out of here, NOW. The fluid was bloody."

I could feel the color drain from my face. Bloody pleural fluid: less likely infection, much higher likelihood of a malignancy. I thought I had steeled myself for this result, but obviously I had been hanging onto the hope that it was not going to be more evidence of cancer. A few days later, at her invitation, a number of us gathered in her living room, and led by a close friend, we offered blessings on Meredith as she faced treatment for what we then knew was a metastatic pleural effusion from her breast cancer. Overnight, stage IV breast cancer indefinitely postponed the "we think you are cured" ten-year anniversary party.

We all wanted to believe she would lick the cancer again. My head said differently; I feared she would be dead in under three years. After a few days of acute fear and maybe terror not shared with others, Meredith got up, and said, "I can do this." Her son was just starting high school and her daughter was in college. "I can do this," meant also living with fear, a fear that sometimes would just be a low-level constant companion and at others a raging terror that would keep her up at night. From our conversations I knew she had a variety of strategies to control her fear. She read, she talked with friends and let us help out, she hoped, she took little trips out of town, sometimes she prayed, and she sought information. The straight scoop helped her always. No sugar coating. She needed to know what was what.

It seemed to her doctors that her best hope at that time was a several-stage treatment. The whole process would take months.

First they gave her initial chemotherapy to see what happened to the pleural effusion. Her tumor responded, and there was no evidence of the effusion on her next CT scan. It was gone! My hope rose. Other blood work and scans did not show evidence of cancer in her bones, lungs, liver, other organs, or blood. The presumption, though, was that cancer cells were there, still lurking in her tissues, too few for our technology to detect, but enough to start quietly multiplying, to eventually show up in an organ, bone, or brain as more metastatic disease. This is where the high-dose chemotherapy came in. At such a toxic dosage, it would hopefully eradicate those elusive cancer cells. At the same time, because these drugs do not discriminate cancer from healthy cells, it would all but kill the healthy cells in her immune system, creating the need for infusion of healthy immune cells provided by a bone marrow transplant.

In advance of high-dose chemo came the harvesting of healthy stem cells, the precursor cells of the immune and blood cell systems that live in bone marrow and turn into all the different blood cells we have, red cells, white cells, and platelets. Mer was given medication to stimulate her bone marrow to produce a surplus of stem cells and to release them into her blood stream. Because the bone marrow is revved up, many people feel pain in their bones during this part of treatment. Meredith dragged her achy body to work anyway. Then she spent several sessions in the infusion center, where she sat for hours while the blood from her body left through intravenous tubing, then coursed through a filter and back into her body. The filtration removed the stem cells, which were prepared for freezing and storage, saving them to later give back to her.

The next phase was the high-dose chemotherapy. This phase left Meredith ill with fevers, nausea, and some infections. She was profoundly weak, barely able to eat or walk to the bathroom. When her blood counts became dangerously low, her marrow essentially dying from the chemotherapy toxicity, she was hospitalized and re-infused with her saved stem cells. Then came her lonely vigil, not wanting to worry her daughter and son. Would the transplant take? Would the stem cells differentiate so her body could re-grow the various types of healthy blood cells she needed? Was the cancer gone? She later told me that during that time, she was sure she was dying.

She didn't die. She came home, her immune system did recover with her new stem cells, and we all were buoyed by her recovery ... tentative but buoyed. Meredith gradually got her strength back and returned to her teaching job. She went on a medication to suppress any lingering cancer cells, while she and her oncology team kept an eye on her symptoms, her scans, and the blood tests that showed her tumor markers. She would celebrate when the markers were low and imaging normal and worry when they increased, hoping along with all of us for new therapies to appear on the horizon in case her current ones lost their effectiveness.

During her recovery from the high-dose chemo and stem cell transplant, a patient of mine, Rosemary, had a recurrence of her breast cancer. Her oncologists were recommending the same treatment Meredith had just completed. Feeling cautiously optimistic from Meredith's story, I offered to connect the two women if Meredith was willing. They had several conversations, and Rosemary went forward with the treatment. Her course was similar but maybe slightly less severe than Meredith's had been. She too returned home and returned to work. Her doctors were ... well, hopeful.

Our optimism was short lived. Within months of both women completing their transplants, new studies showed that this treatment was actually no better than the standard chemotherapy regimens at less toxic doses, without stem cell transplants. Cancer centers all over the country stopped offering this option to patients with metastatic breast cancer.

Rosemary stayed well, with low tumor markers, but also with a bone marrow that never quite fully recovered, leaving her anemic and tired though apparently cancer free. Meredith's tumor markers increased. Initially during the next twelve years, she had intervals of up to a couple of years where she had no clear evidence of cancer and was not on any medication other than suppressive therapy. Those intervals shortened, and she had several recurrences. She changed chemotherapy, had at least two surgeries, changed suppressive therapy, tried new chemotherapy drugs, and kept believing that she could live many years with her cancer, treating it like a chronic disease, not a death sentence.

In between blood counts and new evidence of her cancer, she taught literature to middle school students, mentored new teachers, made new friends and sustained on-going relationships, graduated her son from high school and her daughter from college, fell in love, retired from teaching, attended the weddings of both her son and daughter, welcomed two grand-children, traveled, and celebrated numerous holidays. Often during those years, usually prompted by reading about someone else's death and how the obituary writers phrased things, she would beg, "Oh gawd! Do NOT let anyone say what a great fight I put up, or that I bravely battled the cancer, or any of that garbage. There is nothing noble about cancer."

Meredith died from metastatic breast cancer, and keeping my promise, I will say instead that she lived hopefully. She lived longer than I initially thought or dared to think. She pulled many of us into her version of hope, which for me in this case included the spillover from the personal to the professional in my care of Rosemary.

Chapter 6

Lessons About Control

Diabetes and Other Controls
Sharon Dobie

He is now in his fifties, but when his doctor went on maternity leave and we started to work together, he was in his early thirties. That was just a few months after she told him about the diabetes. He had gone to see her with some blurry vision. His work as a bus mechanic and driver was getting harder because he said he just could not see so well. She sent him to have his eyes and vision evaluated, thinking he probably needed glasses. He was not nearsighted, but his eye doctor was fairly certain it was diabetes. Blood tests confirmed it.

The first time I met him, I opened the door to the exam room to greet a neatly dressed African American man. Big smile, gentle eyes, quiet voice and very much wanting to be healthy, to learn about his diabetes and to not have it take him down. He was not overweight, and we pondered together and with our consultants whether this even was Type II, which tends to unmask in obese persons with a family history of diabetes, or Type I, which usually appears at a younger age. Regardless, we both knew we needed to work to get it under control. Our team formed: him, our nutritionist, our nurse educator, our pharmacist, and me. Our nurse educator and I both taught him about various aspects of self-management of his diabetes. He learned how to stick his finger, put a drop of his blood on a little piece of paper, and insert it into the little handheld machine for reading the blood glucose level. The machine would report that value, and the seven-, fourteen-, and thirty-day averages. He went home from those early sessions with the tools and motivation to collect data that would help us adjust his medications and control his diabetes, or at least his blood sugars.

Mr. B's diabetes is not well controlled. At best, in the years I have been his doctor, it was controlled for six months at a stretch, maybe three or four times. Neither of us seems to be able to figure it out. He is a smart guy yet now, twenty years later, Mr. B's diabetes control is still elusive. Each team member knew their part, and they still do, but the playbook was never fully developed and followed. Initially he took oral medications. When that did not adequately lower his sugars, we added insulin. He still does not tightly control his calories.

Diabetes can and often does affect many parts of our bodies. Mr. B had high blood sugars, he developed high blood pressure within the first year, and he had abnormal vessel formation on the retinas of his eyes. His sugars needed to be controlled. Without good control, and even sometimes with it, a person might face a multitude of problems: high blood pressure, kidney failure, blindness, vascular disease with heart attacks and strokes, numbness and pain in the feet, legs, and hands, slow transit of food through the intestine with nausea and vomiting, sexual dysfunction, skin infections and diseases, and poor healing of wounds, to name just a few.

Besides his high blood pressure and the eye complications, his kidney function is starting to worsen. He tries to regulate his insulin and his eating, but his blood sugar is rarely at the goal level. Over the last seven years, he has gone from normal weight to overweight, and without regular exercise, this is complicating his sugar control efforts. He works hard as a bus driver on the swing shift. When he can eat and what he can eat is not predictable. That makes regulation of his insulin challenging. In an attempt to avoid episodes of hypoglycemia, or his sugars being too low, most of them are too high. Control evades us.

He has some aches and pains that are job related, but overall he feels pretty well. He knows his visual symptoms are best controlled when his glucometer readings are normal. He does not otherwise "feel" his high sugars, his worsening kidney function, whatever is happening in his arteries from his high blood pressure, nor any of what might be silently brewing problems with his heart. What would it take to control his diabetes? What would control give him?

Normalizing his sugars would require diet management and insulin adjustment, especially with regular meals, and daily calls or emails for a week or two with our diabetes nurse or me. During those conversations we would change his insulin dose based on the glucometer readings, on what he had eaten before, and on what he planned to eat at that meal. In talking through all this with him, he would be learning more, so he could adjust his insulin dose on his own. More exercise and some weight loss would also help normalize his sugars. Mr. B sometimes commits to doing these things, including following through with email or phone conversations with our nurse. He sticks with it for a week, maybe two, and then he is gone. A month or several will go by, and then he will return for a visit about a new concern, for the checkup he needs for his license, or about his diabetes. We have repeat conversations as I search for new ideas that might work to get us where he needs to be: in control—of his glucose and other things.

"Mr. B, what do you think is in the way of tighter control of your diabetes?"

"I don't know," he always responds, although recently his voice is more quiet, his brow a bit more furrowed. What am I hearing in his voice?

"I'm starting to get worried. What does the prospect of dialysis mean to you?"

"I'm really scared these days that I'll get sick. I don't want to need dialysis, ever."

He tries to look at what is in the way of changing his approach and engaging more with managing his diabetes. He cannot really pinpoint the barriers, and my work with him has identified his fears, but not a path towards changing his diabetes control. He recommits, emails back and forth a few times, and then does not call and is not available when we call him. And so it goes. I cannot get enough of the pattern of his sugars to really make solid recommendations.

I realize he is really afraid of becoming sicker, but what changes? He has seen the kidney doctors, the diabetes doctors, the liver doctors. And little changes. Me? I keep thinking there has to be a way. Why can't I find the key?

If he would stick a bit longer with any plan we lay out, would we figure out his eating pattern and come up with a better way for him to titrate his insulin? Whenever he comes for a visit, I bring up his diabetes control. I evaluate my recommendations and adjust them based on the priorities we set in the visit. Sometimes I wonder if he thinks I am a broken record. He, however, gets to decide. I try to lower my expectations and not my hopes. I do not get to have it "my way." Ultimately, he decides. In any case, the impact of our work together is not just about his glucose control, and I may never know what the impact is. Reminding myself that there might be effects that I simply cannot appreciate, I carry on.

When my children were little, I could fasten their seat belts, put healthy food on the table, and send them to school. I could tie privileges – playing with a friend or TV – to chore or homework completion. Even then, parental control was an illusion and expectations were tricky. Now that my sons are adults, I recognize even more clearly how limited my role is. And what about me? What percentage of the time do I eat what I should, avoid what I should avoid, exercise, and get enough sleep?

I wonder if working with Mr. B gives me useful practice in understanding the imperfections and limits of control—his, mine, everyone's. I have spent years working with patients, and when I say, "I think you have this infection and need antibiotics," most patients will agree and take some, if not all, of the medication. Sometimes it is more complicated. I might want to do testing or a treatment that runs counter to what the patient thinks and wants, or a patient might want testing or treatment that I do not think is warranted. Either way, one visit or many visits lead to decisions and agreements between a patient and me.

Most personality types are represented among health care providers. Neither those who are tolerant of patient autonomy nor those who prefer control are immune from the fact that there is a lot, in practice and in life, that we do not control. In the following narratives, physicians describe ways that the dance of collaboration and control affected them, times when they recognized that control was not theirs and then reflected on what they could learn about themselves.

The Reverend

Anthony Suchman

A 64-year-old retired minister and professor was seeking help for anxiety symptoms; they related to a fear of strong winds that started when he and his wife lived through a hurricane, huddling in a closet as their house blew down around them. An acquaintance referred him to see me. He hadn't seen a doctor in many years, and it turned out that he had a fear of doctors, and of medical care, too. In our introductory telephone conversation I let him know that he could decline the usual preparatory routines for our office visits that heightened his anxiety (measuring his blood pressure and weight and so forth); that may have been what convinced him to come see me.

We spent our first visit talking at some length about his work and life, his experience in the hurricane, and his subsequent anxiety symptoms. Having deferred until a future date the usual routine of the complete physical exam, at the end of the visit I asked if I could at least measure his blood pressure. He agreed. As I took the reading, I was dismayed to discover that it was quite elevated—210/110. This would be hard news for him to hear. I recognized that my own sense of responsibility and fear of an untoward outcome made me want to head straight into a complete work-up and prompt pharmacologic treatment, preferably right then and there. But such an aggressive approach would likely scare him off, and he'd end up with no treatment at all.

So he and I took a slightly more measured pace. He bought a home blood pressure kit so he could take his own readings at home and at work and get used to the procedure. Bringing in readings that were elevated, he agreed to start treatment in the next week, and he even had a first round of blood tests. He also started taking a medication for anxiety, though I still wasn't able to do a complete "history and physical." But we'll get there.

I am aware how much my practice routines address my own anxiety; it was a great learning opportunity to set those aside in serving the patient's unique experience and needs. Gaining his gratitude and trust was rewarding to me, and a chance to feel skilled—like I was just the right doctor for him. That doesn't happen very often.

I bring some compulsiveness and an attitude of "it has to be done exactly this way" to circumstances outside of medicine. It's a way of maintaining a sense of order and calm—in things like packing for a vacation, or planning out a day or how certain tasks get done around the house. When my wife or children have other ideas about how something should be arranged, I can sometimes stop and think about the effect that my inflexibility would have on them. In that moment, collaborating harmoniously with them becomes more important than whatever comfort would have come from imposing my own preferred sense of order. But regardless of context, this is really a matter of being mindful of my own anxiety, the behaviors it elicits, and how these affect others.

Despite Our Predictions

Amy Rodriguez

Mrs. T was an 85-year-old woman I cared for on the medicine service. She had been in the Trauma Intensive Care Unit (TICU) following a motor vehicle accident that resulted in a punctured lung and bleeding into her chest cavity. She had been in the TICU for days, initially on the ventilator, and she had a chest tube to drain the air and blood from her chest cavity and to help her lung re-expand.

Her two daughters and her son spent a lot of time at her bedside. Prior to the accident, she lived in an assisted living facility. One of her daughters lived nearby and was very involved socially with her, and one lived in another state, but flew home when the accident happened. Mrs. T's son, who also lived locally, had Power of Attorney to make decisions for her. She was "full code," meaning that if her respiratory status changed or if her heart stopped, we would be asked to do all resuscitation measures available to us, including intubation again, or shocking her heart.

The patient's prognosis looked pretty grim. She needed a lot of high flow oxygen through a full facemask and was being fed by a nasogastric tube from her nose to her stomach because she was not strong enough to swallow. The nasogastric feeding tube is only a short-term way to deliver nutrition. The alternative is called a PEG (percutaneous endoscopic gastrostomy) tube and is a feeding tube inserted directly from skin to stomach. Putting one in is a procedure that requires sedation and is more risky than the nasogastric tube. The former, however, would need to be pulled within days. Because of her frailty, age, and prognosis, we did not think it was ethical to put her through a procedure to insert a PEG tube. She had a lung that was not fully expanded because of slowly accumulated fluid, but because she was very weak the surgeons did not want to put in another chest tube.

I was an intern on a team with several interns, a senior resident, an attending doctor, and a social worker. We did not think she would survive her injuries, and we shared this with her children several times. There were nearly daily bedside discussions about her. As her intern, I would go to see her every morning before rounds with the team. In addition to examining her and checking her vital signs and lab values, I would talk with the family. Usually it was the two daughters who were with her in those early morning hours. There were a lot of tears. "How was she so badly injured and I was hardly hurt at all?" asked her local daughter, the driver of the car. "It just seems so unfair." Her other daughter's guilt was for living so far away.

I encouraged them to think about what the best and kindest direction of her care would be, that would also correspond with what they thought their mother would want. Mrs. T was awake briefly during the day but was unable to communicate her wishes. I remained certain she was not going to survive the accident.

Despite the poor prognosis, I tempered my words to them. "She's not doing very well. She still needs a lot of oxygen and that is not a good sign. Because of her age, she is recovering less quickly, and being so severely injured, she may not be able to recover at all."

This would bring more tears, "But she will recover slowly. She might get better."

"That is possible, but the likelihood of her recovering fully is not very good." I would continue. "While some older people might feel they would want to try everything possible to keep going, others reach a certain time in their life where they feel they have lived a full life and would not want to continue treatments to prolong their lives if it were going to be painful or hard. What kind of person is your mom?"

They were not able to answer that question and stuck to their original answer. "There is no way we can give up on her. If there's a chance, we want to continue all treatment."

The team visited the patient and her family on rounds, and though these visits were brief, the content echoed my early morning visits. The team thought she should be placed on "comfort care," which means many interventions (following lab values, drawing blood, and taking frequent vital signs) would stop. Placing someone on comfort care is a statement of expectation that the person is dying, or at least not likely to be helped by the acute care our doctors and hospital offer. The team also believed this was a decision the family needed to make, with our medical guidance. Mrs. T's daughters were present often, and they freely shared their feelings of guilt. Her son was less outwardly emotional about his thought process, but it was clear that all three were jointly making the decision to continue all treatment.

So we did.

The pictures of this once vibrant, stylish woman posted above the bedside stayed with me even when I'd left the room or the hospital for the day.

Despite the grim picture and our advice, this patient did heal very slowly over time. I had moved on to another rotation and she was ultimately discharged, after more than a month, to the full care nursing section of her assisted living home. I saw her several months later in the emergency department. I was there to admit another patient; she was there for an unrelated and minor problem. Her daughters saw me and called me over.

I did not immediately recognize them out of context and partly because Mrs. T looked so different. She looked like the woman in the pictures on the wall of her hospital room from several months earlier. Her voice was back and she was actually a little feisty, joking and asserting her opinion about her current care.

I had a chance to come in and chat briefly, and was really happy to see how well she was doing. And even though I had once suggested that we not provide heroic treatment to their mom and was proved wrong, they were happy to see me and remarked how happy they were with their mom's care after that horrible accident.

We see families during their most memorable times in their lives, even though it may be part of the day-to-day grind for us. This family taught me to support family and patient decisions that may not entirely jibe with what I feel is best. The outcome may be very different from what we expect or are trained to predict.

Just as this experience taught me that it is important to really hear what the patient and their family say about their wishes, it also taught me about differences of opinions, avoiding snap judgments, and keeping an open mind. We predict so we can have some control over how things will go. Yet, how good are we at predicting, really?

Personal Choice
Roger Rosenblatt

Way back in the 1970s I was an intern on what was then called Blue Medicine Service, the most acute of medical wards in a university hospital. There were no ICUs in those days. Interns admitted people, did medical workups, and took care of them. Of all who were on the team, interns got to know their patients the best. One day, about three months into my internship, an elderly gentleman quite ill from sepsis, a serious bacterial infection in the blood, was admitted to my service. He had gotten the infection because of his underlying leukemia and was very ill with a high fever. My residents, the doctors in training who were senior to me, guided me in evaluating him; we obtained a blood culture and started an IV with antibiotics. Luckily, his infection cleared up within 72 hours.

In caring for this man, as an intern I was not paying much attention to anything but the rapid beating of my own heart. For me, it would have been quite enough to get the IV going, solve the immediate problem, and see him out the door. Still, I tried to make time every day to sit down on the patient's bed and just spend a couple of minutes talking with him and his son. It gave them a chance to ask questions, and it fed my need for a human connection. During one of these talks, I found out that my patient was still living alone in a semi-rural area. His wife had died, and his son, a physician, lived close by and was very involved in his life. My patient's questions showed he also had an interest in me. In his soft voice, he asked how I was doing as an intern and inquired about my work, my life, and my studies.

As I think back, I realize he cared for me, was interested in my development as a human being and a physician. He asked his questions seriously, and in a gentle, non-didactic way he was almost paternal in his comments and responses. I was in my 20's, for heaven's sake, and incredibly green. His son, a man in his 40s or 50s, was often there as well, asking good questions about his dad's care and listening to his dad explore my life with me.

He finished his antibiotics, and we discharged him back to his home in the country. About a week later, he reappeared, again septic and maybe a little sicker than the first time. I asked if I could be his intern again and my resident agreed; we went through the same medical drill, picking up where we had left off. This time the culture came back as pseudomonas, a much more virulent and dangerous infection, and in those days virtually untreatable. The antibiotics we could use on pseudomonas were toxic, and even with them many patients died from the infection. With leukemia afflicting the patient as well, it would be only a temporary treatment anyway.

"Well," I said, "we are going to treat you the same as before." But I didn't disclose much—we didn't tell patients much in those days.

"Before you do that," he said, "can I talk to my son, just the two of us?" His son was in the room listening, and I left, saying I'd come back in half an hour.

When I returned, they were packing up his clothes. I was aghast. I turned to the father and son and said, "You don't understand. I don't know what you're doing. This is a really dangerous infection, a bug called pseudomonas, what they call a gram negative."

"You know, it's okay, doctor," responded the son, very gently. "I'm the chairman of the microbiology department and I know all about pseudomonas."

Then his father, my patient, said, "I realize that this is really not a disease I'm going to survive. And I want to go home. I have a special little room that overlooks the valley and the river below it and want to just spend my remaining time, whatever that is, in that room and be visited by my family."

It flabbergasted me because we would never think of that as an option. For us, the disease was the enemy and we were the shock troops—we were going to fight it! It never occurred to us that patients might actually prefer not to. There was no such thing as palliative care, end-of-life care, or even hospices 40 years ago. I didn't even think people were allowed to choose to refuse medical care, especially if it meant that they might die as a result. But when I thought about it for a moment, it made sense and it was obvious that this patient was making the right decision for himself and for the rest of us.

My resident and the rest of the team were also quite supportive. And so I helped him pack his things, gave him a hug, and he went home. About a week later I got a wonderful, loving call from his son. "I just wanted to let you know that my Dad passed away peacefully, sitting in his favorite rocking chair, and with no pain. And I want to thank you for your understanding."

That relationship completely recalibrated my core orientation to what we were doing and my place within it. The right to decline care had never been brought up in medical school or in several months of internship. It was really the patient and his son who taught me that there was such a thing as choosing one's own path through end-of-life care.

After this, I spent a lot more time sitting on patients' beds and talking with them—as much for me as for them. I enjoyed sitting with patients, being part of their lives, and having them be part of mine.

That relationship seeded a total paradigm shift. It affected the way my brothers and I chose to take care of my father in the terminal phases of Alzheimer's and the decision to not treat his pneumonia at the end of his life. It also affected my decisions about a friend who got Alzheimer's and asked for end-of-life assistance. This story is still very salient, very powerful to me. It completely changed my approach to taking care of patients with lethal or very severe diseases, and to taking care of myself.

When We Cannot Fix

Anonymous

He was a vet who saw combat, and like so many vets, he also had Post-Traumatic Stress Disorder. But it was NASH, not PTSD that brought him to the hospital: non-alcoholic steatohepatitis, also called fatty liver. The bottom line was that his liver was failing. There are many ramifications to this condition. One has to do with ammonia, a breakdown product from our food that should be excreted through stool. In people with liver failure, it builds up in the blood and is toxic to the brain. This man was in his early 60s, and off and on for years he had suffered from bouts of confusion, or "altered mental status," from his liver disease and this ammonia build-up. He would be confused and not able to put clear thoughts together; sometimes he hallucinated, and at times he would lose his memory.

We call that kind of confusion a form of delirium, specifically hepatic encephalopathy. Because of these episodes, he was living in a skilled nursing facility, visited by his wife daily. Several times a month, he was admitted to the hospital for treatment. He was given lactulose at incredible doses, by mouth and per rectum. The lactulose would act in a couple of ways to help chemicals in the intestine convert ammonia so it could not be absorbed; the inevitable diarrhea carries the accumulated ammonia out in the stool. Once the patient's ammonia level was lowered, he would wake up and go back to the nursing home.

I met him during one of his usual admissions. But this time it was not going to be usual. We examined him and determined that he was delirious and in dire need of lactulose. His delirium left him unable to make decisions, and we had to rely on his wife to know his wishes. We took her aside to discuss his code status. He was noted to be full code on all prior admissions, and I wonder in retrospect how often this couple had been asked about their wishes. To our surprise, his wife not only wanted him to be DNR/DNI (do not resuscitate/do not intubate), she also requested him to not be actively treated. She requested that we put him on a morphine drip to numb his delirious agitation so he would not have to suffer anymore. We call this "comfort care." Not knowing the patient or his wife, or their relationship, this seemed rather strange to me. Having gone through this before, they both should have known that the altered mental status was reversible with the lactulose.

I sat down with her the next day to discuss her husband's condition at length. Just like all the other times, he needed the lactulose to clear his mental status. There was nothing different about his condition this time that would make him less likely to improve again–at least, nothing that we could find. That we cannot always know something is different would prove to be truer than I ever imagined.

She agreed to the lactulose treatment, and we believed his mind would clear if he got some lactulose into his gut. So we put a nasogastric tube down his nose into his stomach and a rectal tube from below. He pulled the tubes out. Figuring that he did not have decision-making capacity in his current mental status and that his behavior was actively harming him, we put him in five-point restraints. I shiver at the awful power displayed by restraining someone, even when it is strictly used only if someone is hurting himself or herself. In this case, it did not make a difference. To the huge despair of the nurses, no matter what we did he managed to pull out his rectal and nasogastric tubes, or he vomited whatever lactulose we got in.

He kept telling me, "Leave me alone," and "Take this away." These were the only understandable words he ever mouthed in that hospitalization, and they came between the moaning and agitation. Later I learned of something else that he kept saying that I did not understand. His wife told us it sounded like the name of his long deceased father. Although he was completely delirious and not considered capable of making any decisions for himself, I still wonder how much these statements reflected the patient's true wishes. If his thinking had been clear, would he have had the same desire that he was uttering in the only clear words he said? In the end, despite all of our attempts, we were unable to get the lactulose into him.

After three days, his wife and our team of physicians decided to try no longer; we transitioned him to comfort care. This is a difficult decision when a patient does not have the mental capacity to state their wishes, and particularly when the patient has a condition that is believed to be reversible. But it was consistent with his wife's expressed desires, and it was clear that she tried to reflect his wishes to the best of her ability. After the nasogastric and rectal tubes were removed, he finally slept peacefully.

His agitation was gone and he did not wake up for visitors or nursing care, with two exceptions. Even at places like a VA hospital, compassion can win over rules and regulations, and his wife was allowed to bring in his little dog and put it on his chest. Having not been awake for days, and with his dog on his chest, he briefly opened his eyes and lifted his head off the pillow before falling back into his comatose state. When his eight-year-old niece came by and sang him a song holding his hand, she suddenly exclaimed, "He squeezed my hand!"

The next day, he died. When his American flag wrapped casket rolled by through the hallway, I pondered how little we really understand about what is going on in the mind of an unconscious person, no matter whether the loss of consciousness was because of sickness, medications or the approaching end of life. At the same time I marveled at how much human beings and their closest friends, partner, or family know about what is best and when death is near.

We held to our thoughts that it was incomprehensible that his wife requested that her husband be placed on comfort care from the beginning of his hospitalization, even though she had acquiesced and let us try to treat her husband. But while we were making an effort to be patient with her and giving her time to learn and understand our medical logic, it turned out she was giving us time to understand that medical logic might fail and that there are limits to what we can know and do. The deep connection she had with her husband over all those years contained information that is not amenable to the logic or clinical reasoning found in a medical textbook. It was an unforgettable lesson for me about the depth and importance of human relationships, as well as of the limits of control or the powers of logic and reasoning.

My scientific mind still wonders how his wife could have known that admission was going to be her husband's last. And how, in spite of what seemed to be a deep coma, was he able to say the words "Take this away"? How could he purposefully move his head, eyes, and hand in the presence of his beloved dog and his singing niece? It was an experience that increased my sense of the privilege of being a physician. Participating in such stories widens my horizon and my appreciation of life more than I can know or articulate. I notice more, accept more without explanation, and allow myself to be amazed.

Not Trying
Sharon Dobie

He weighs over 300 pounds. He is unkempt when I see him, with un-washed hair, slumped in the chair, his long face and words telling me how miserable his life is. "I'm depressed," he says. "I would be fine if I could just get this weight fixed. That's what depresses me." But he won't take an antidepressant and won't see a counselor. He says he copes with life by eating. He wants gastric bypass surgery, but he can't qualify unless he diets for at least six months, exercises, and loses at least 40 pounds.

He is not doing it: no diet, no exercise, no effort. "I can't do it. It's making me more depressed to not have the surgery. It's not my fault," he says, eyes downward. "All my family is overweight. It's genetic."

"Do any of them weigh as much as you?" I ask.

"No, but they don't have my wife cooking for them."

Everything is externalized; he is the victim. Maybe he was victimized at some time, but I can't get him talking about his life. All I hear is how he won't try. Actually, he uses "can't" much more than "won't."

He is dying. His weight will kill him. I don't know if it will be diabetes, or an early heart attack, maybe a stroke. I can do little more than watch, continue to offer my ideas, try to come up with new ideas that won't be ignored or rejected, and not walk away, try to keep listening.

I don't think I want to make anyone do anything. Maybe I do, though. Why do I continue to think if I cheerlead the good life, others will respond? It's what I do with some family and friends, too, even though I am not perfect in my own choices. There are habits I should break, and don't. But it's hard to watch and let someone else slowly self-destruct. At least that's how it looks from where I sit, feeling no power over the situation.

Why Didn't She?
Sharon Dobie

She walked into clinic to see me. "Doc, we need to talk about this growth in my stomach. And I'm short of breath." She was an artist who also worked in a café to make ends meet. In her mid-fifties, she lived in our clinic's neighborhood, and I had not seen her in clinic for several years.

When she lifted up her shirt, I could hear her heart pounding in her chest—too fast, I thought. Her shallow breathing also seemed fast, and there was a bulge in her abdomen. I was not sure if the bulge was fluid (ascites), or a mass. When I examined her, it was clear it was ascites, her belly full of so much fluid she looked 9 months pregnant, with twins.

"Dear Lord! How long have you noticed that?"

It was impossible to hide my dismay. My mind was reeling with questions. What was causing this ascites? Why was she short of breath? Is the fluid pushing her diaphragm up, making it hard for her to take a full breath? What if this is even worse, a cancer that has already spread to her lungs? What took her so long to come in? Was it her beliefs, or fear, or something else? She was not a believer in allopathic (my kind of) medicine. She usually went to a faith healer and a naturopathic doctor. When she came to see me in clinic, it was usually for something acute, like a urinary tract infection. Occasionally she came for a checkup, although she never wanted screening tests. She only got around to having mammograms every three years or so, and never got her colon cancer screening.

My jaw dropped at her response.

"I saw my naturopath about six months ago, who thinks it's a lymphoma. Well he thinks it is a cancer anyway. He said lymphoma would be best because that relates to my immune system cells and is treatable. He did a chest X-Ray and everything and saw something there, too. He said medical doctors, not naturopathic doctors, needed to treat this and told me to come back to you. He called me a month later to see if I had, and again said that I should see you. He did give me some herbs to keep my immune system up and said they might help if I had to go through treatment. I figured since he thought it was lymphoma, the immune system herbs he gave me should take care of it. Thing is, it seems to keep growing, and the breathing is getting to me."

She agreed to a CT scan and it showed tumors in her lungs and liver. She was then willing to step into my medical world for biopsies, surgery, and chemotherapy, which continued until she died, just two years after her diagnosis. I felt guilty when she was diagnosed, as if I could have done more to nudge her towards the philosophy of screening I preach.

I try to influence my patients, sometimes with more pressure than other times, and I wonder what influences the amount of pressure I bring to a conversation – really, to any topic – with patients or friends. How do we know when to push to get our way, force an action, try to control a situation? How do we decide when to step back? What is too much? Too little?

Mohel to the Rescue

Sharon Dobie

I have cared for many young couples having their first baby. I remember one couple in my practice when I was a second-year resident physician in family medicine. I had been the woman's physician before she got pregnant, provided her prenatal care, delivered their son, and was her husband's physician as well. Not knowing their child's gender before the birth, I provided my usual and typical education about circumcision.

"Let's talk about circumcision," I said in one clinic visit. "Have you thought about whether you want one if you have a boy?" The couple said, "We don't know. What do you think?"

I probably said something similar to the following: "They're not medically necessary. It is a valid cosmetic, cultural, or religious choice, and not a medical choice. It's low risk but not without risk. I do them, and I do them well; I've never had a complication. And I don't think they are necessary." I then would have explained the procedure and its risks, including bleeding, infection, and penile injury.

At the time, I hoped to sway families away from the circumcision procedure unless they had cultural or religious reasons for choosing it. In the case of this couple, after the birth of their son they declined the procedure and I discharged the infant boy from the hospital without a circumcision.

Imagine my surprise when they brought him in for his well-child exam at two weeks of age and he was circumcised! Almost before the diaper was off and my jaw dropped, both parents blushed. "We know you don't believe in circumcisions, and we didn't want to put you in the position of having to perform one," the dad said. Although they were not Jewish, they had hired a mohel, the specially trained person who performs the bris, or circumcision, on male Jewish infants. Their gesture was touching, and very embarrassing.

Should I say less to my patients who wanted circumcisions for their newborns? At a minimum, this family had perceived my feelings differently than I intended. While I wanted them to make their own decision, this family taught me to realize the force of my words and the subtle ways I may seek to control. What appears inside my head as my words in muted colors might, out in the world, actually appear as words painted in bold primary colors. Even now, many years later, it is work to hear how my communications are received, how I present information and myself. I know not to assume that what is being heard is necessarily what I intend to be heard.

The Ripple Effect
Sharon Dobie

Sunny lived with her partner in a two-room cabin in the woods, down an overgrown trail. They had a wood stove, no electricity, no phone, and no running water. It was 1976 and they were "off the grid" because they wanted to be. They occasionally worked in town and as part of a tree-planting collective. And when we met, they were about to become parents. She was about twenty, with coveralls and t-shirt over her very pregnant belly and what used to be blond hair now in brown braids down her back, curly strands escaping their entire length. He did not seem much older—tall, lanky, the calloused hands of hard work. They had been together a couple of years,

I was between the first and second years of medical school, spending the summer working in a rural clinic and living on the communal farm that was home for most of the providers and other clinic staff. When I was not gardening or cooking on the farm, I was seeing patients with the physician and midwives. It was on one of those days that I met Sunny and her partner.

This was her first pregnancy, and the two of them were grinning with excitement when I entered the room. They told me they were ready for a home birth in their cabin. They had done our midwives' birthing classes and were ready for natural childbirth. The plan was for a lay midwife to attend her birth, with our doctor coming towards the end of labor as he always did. Someone would fetch the team when labor started. The couple's car was parked at the trailhead near their cabin whenever Sunny was home.

On the day I met her, Sunny was near her due date – "at term," or 40 weeks of gestation, we would say. Because she had a history of herpes, we asked her if she had any new sores. She reluctantly admitted to some, and our exam showed a cluster of small ulcers, confirming what looked like active herpes lesions.

Neonatal herpes is rare but dangerous. The fetus can contract it through the placenta before labor and birth, but most contract it by coming in contact with the virus during a vaginal delivery. The risk to a newborn is worse if a pregnant woman has a first bout of herpes close to her due date, but the recommendation was (and still is) to have a caesarian section if the woman has active sores when labor starts, even if they are from a recurrent bout.

We discussed this with her and talked about setting up her delivery in town with one of the obstetricians. With planning, we preferred to work with an obstetrician two hospitals away, a drive of about an hour and a half. He was more accepting of our patients, a mix of low-income rural farmers and commune dwellers. For emergencies, patients were taken to the nearest town with a hospital, about fifty minutes away. For Sunny, we hoped for an arranged operation at the further hospital and were ready to call and set a date.

She said "No." No discussion. Just "No." The advice from our side was lengthy and included her midwife and then the physician, working to convince her to go to town for a C-Section. They explained that babies with neonatal herpes can suffer seizures and coma and, if they live, permanent brain damage. Yes, they can die. Thanks to more rapid treatment, the mortality from neonatal herpes has dropped to about 25% in this country, but at the time of Sonny's pregnancy, upwards of 75% of babies with this condition did not survive. Sunny and her partner, Robert, were given that statistic. Nothing changed Sunny's mind. She said she did not like hospitals; she was afraid of them.

"I know my baby will be ok," she added. She gave no reason for her fear, nor did we unearth any history to explain it. Our clinic served many people who had left the mainstream and "dropped out" for many different reasons. I didn't know hers, only that she was adamant that she would not go to the hospital. Robert did not argue with her.

At the end of each day, our entire staff would meet together. Sometimes it was on the clinic porch, sometimes inside, sometimes down at the river. But what we did was the same: we reviewed every patient seen that day. The discussions focused on the medical concerns of each patient and often included teaching. When it was time to discuss Sunny, the question was about how to proceed. Should we attend the birth or not? If we didn't, would that prompt her to go to the hospital? What would happen if she didn't go to the hospital and they delivered their baby by themselves? How would she fare if there were complications, with no medical assistance and so far from the hospital? What if this baby was born infected and ill and needed transport to the hospital? What if valuable time was lost coming to get our medical team for the transport?

My thoughts were all over the place. First off, I wanted her to take the expert advice of my supervising doctor and midwives. My mouth had been open, gaping, when she insisted she would not go to the hospital for her delivery. How could she say no? How could she take this risk with her baby? As the day wore on, I felt irritated with her. It started to feel personal. Her decision was going to weigh on all of us, no matter how it played out. By the time I got to the riverbank review of the day, I had talked myself into and out of every possible response to her – no, our – situation.

The group believed that Sunny would not change her mind even if she heard the team was not coming and that the risk was too great to have her deliver without medical attention. They decided to attend the birth.

The clinic had a phone and a radio connection to the farm. Someone was on site at the clinic 24 hours a day. The van, with a transport incubator, was kept in decent running condition and stocked, including a pack of supplies for walking into homes that set off the road. Back at the farm, the midwife on call and the physician each had radios. When a woman went into labor, a family would notify the staff at the clinic, either in person or by phone. If it were after-hours, the person staying at the clinic would radio both the midwife and the physician. The midwife might go first, with the physician coming later, closer to the actual delivery, or they might leave together to attend the birth. I did not need a radio. They knew where to find me. On clear nights I was in the meadow under the stars. On rainy nights, I was in the loft above Daisy, the cow.

Sunny went into labor a few nights later. The midwife on call, the physician, and I loaded up the van, drove to their trailhead, parked, and walked the short distance to their home. The cabin was dimly lit with lanterns and felt warm from the fire in the stove. Sunny was laboring on their bed, propped up by her partner. Her midwife went to work getting ready for the delivery, offering breathing suggestions while she worked, and checking the heart rate of the baby between each contraction with the manual feto-scope.

This was maybe the fourth delivery I had attended in my life, but my midwife teacher-role-models had taught me how to coach a woman in labor, working with her partner. I assumed my position at her side just as she reached that rough spot of being about seven centimeters dilated. Knowing that if she were to give in to her urge to push, she might tear her cervix, I gave her breathing strategies.

"Look at Robert."

"I can't."

"You can. Open your eyes and look at Robert."

"Good, now both of you breathe like this: hee hee hee hee, oh oh oh oh, hee hee hee hee, oh oh oh oh," and I kept demonstrating the rhythm of four hees and four audible short blows of air through my lips.

She and Robert got into the rhythm for a few contractions, but she started to lose it again, with the telltale grunt of a push. I switched rhythms, made sure she watched Robert so he could demonstrate and do the new rhythm with her while I talked them through each contraction. After each contraction, she would lie back, her midwife would check the baby's heart rate, and I would ask Sunny to take a few deep, relaxing breaths. She was particularly good at resting between contractions, letting me take her through a visualization exercise the midwives had taught me to use. By the time she was fully dilated, and ready to push, I was enjoying myself, in no small part because I had been given something to do—something that I could do. Everyone in the room was together, acting synchronously in a well-conducted piece.

Sunny and her midwife delivered her baby son and placed him up on her chest for Robert to cut the umbilical cord. I don't remember if she needed stitches, but I have a mental picture of a bucolic scene: mother, father, and baby wrapped in blankets, cuddled together on a rough-hewn bed. I remember the baby's first latch on the breast, the warm glow of lanterns, wood crackling in the stove, a doctor and a midwife quietly cleaning up and packing supplies. And in some parallel universe was the collective wondering, "is this baby going to get neonatal herpes?"

We examined the baby, and he seemed healthy, but the onset of herpes contracted during birth might not be apparent for two weeks. Making no promises other than to see them the next day on a routine home visit to check on mom and baby, we departed. A quiet walk back up the trail and van ride back to the farm brought us home by midday, ready for a nap.

Later that day, the radio went off. Sunny and Robert were terrified. Now that her baby was born and they were holding him, they were shaken and frightened by the risk she had taken. She was wishing she'd had a caesarian delivery. That day, someone went over to see her, re-examine the baby, and talk with them. For a number of days after that, there were frequent checks and reassurances while we waited to see if this baby developed herpes. Everyone involved lived those days with fear, and many of us wondered if we had done what was best for Sunny, Robert, and their baby. We had let her make her own decision even though it was in stark contradiction to what we recommended. We could have told her that if she did not do as we said, we would not be involved in her birth. But in this case the midwives and physician did not back away. Once Sunny made her choice and assumed the risk, we stayed in the game, so to speak.

What a lesson. Sometimes as a teacher I have a choice: let my student or resident do something their way or insist on my way. Experiences like my relationship with Sunny are instructive in developing a sense of what is mine to control, of what is not, and of the acts of both letting loose the reins of control and not walking away from the situation or person. I don't think we ever got to decide what we would do in a similar future situation; I doubt we would know unless we were there again. That baby did not get neonatal herpes, and I do know that Sunny, at least at that time, said if she had active lesions in a future pregnancy, she would have a caesarian.

How I feel about patients being in control ranges from relief that it is not all my responsibility and comfort in their autonomy, to guilt when the outcome is poor and I wonder if I should have pressed harder, done more. Ceding control to patients or simply not controlling others requires knowing what is ours and what is another's. There is a line, often diffuse, mobile, and undefined between those two loci of responsibility. What is there to learn about that line? How do we come to understand, define, and respect boundaries?

Chapter 7

Where Do We Draw the Line?

Stretched Boundaries

Sharon Dobie

"Roberta is on the bathroom floor. I found her in a pool of blood; she vomited and she won't let me call an ambulance."

"Is she conscious?" I was startled awake from a deep sleep by the phone call from Roberta's sister. Was I even on call? No, Rich was. Why didn't she call 9-1-1?

"Yes, she is conscious."

"Can you give her the phone?"

Roberta worked in our community health center, and like most of us staff, she also got her health care there. She was in her 50s and looked older. I figured that life before I knew her had not been easy. But at the center she was a treasured outreach worker, supporting vulnerable young families and elders with her visits, care, and counsel. She did not mince words with any of us, and all five feet four inches and maybe 100 pounds of her were fierce, advocating for services for our patients. On any given day she could be found trimming toenails of a 90 year-old, doing prenatal screening with a pregnant mom, or giving rides to some of our patients so they would come to their appointments. She let us all know that she more or less tolerated the two of us physicians in the clinic, and she did not really trust us, preferring to get her own care from our nurse practitioners and physician assistants. She scared me, and I never wanted to cross her. That night when she was on the floor, too weak to get up, would be my challenge.

"I'm not going to any hospital. I don't want tests. I don't want surgery. You cannot make me go and you know that," Roberta told me, the words tumbling out as her voice rose in volume.

I pulled any persuasive explanations I could think of out of my pajama pocket. "Roberta, this is probably no big deal. They just need to be sure you did not lose too much blood. I can't tell from what your sister is describing."

"She told you I lost a lot. It's all over the floor."

"It might be something as simple as a bleeding ulcer that needs to be cauterized to stop the bleeding," I tried again, "but without checking you could have more bleeding, more serious complications. You could even die." Even the "you might die" card did not budge her.

"I am not going to die in the hospital."

"No one said anything about dying…"

"Yes you did, and if I'm dying, I will do it in my own bed." I was getting nowhere. But ultimately it would be her choice.

"My sister is going to clean me up and put me to bed and we will see where we are tomorrow." That was as far into the future as she was willing to go.

"OK," I advised her sister, "I think you should call 9-1-1." Her sister was unwilling to cross Roberta, only to have her send the medics away, but she did agree to phone for an ambulance if she vomited again. "Call me if you call 9-1-1, or she changes her mind," I said, and ended the conversation with a promise to call in the morning if I had not heard from them.

When I got off the phone, I started circling my room, fully awake now and thinking. Roberta had the right to choose whether to be hospitalized, but that night I sensed that fear was the leading edge of her choice. And just as importantly, I did not think I could live with her choice. I called her back. She was in clean nightclothes and comfortable in bed.

"I am asking you again to go to the hospital."

"No." was her one-word answer.

"Are you maybe afraid, afraid of the tests, afraid of what they will find?" I asked. "Yes," came her answer, with choked tears, "afraid of what they might find." I again told her the likelihood that they would find an ulcer that they could treat and that she would have the right to refuse treatment at any point. "I know you're afraid," I said, "and it's scary." Sticking my neck out further, I went on. "You have two choices. Call 9-1-1 and get transported to the hospital or I will come over and call 9-1-1. If you refuse their transport, I will put you in my car and take you to the hospital. Either way, one of us will be with you in the Emergency Room."

She took the first option, and my colleague on call met her and her sister at the emergency room. She needed to have an emergency upper endoscopy, where they look down into the esophagus, stomach and first part of the intestine. They found the bleeding ulcer and cauterized it to stop the bleeding. After transfusions, a second procedure to cauterize the bleeding area, and an intensive-care unit stay, she went home.

Incidentally, on that admission, a chest X-Ray revealed a small spot on her lung. It was cancer. Even though this was part of the outcome, and what she had feared, she remained glad that she went to the ER the night of her bleeding ulcer. She went on to live for a few years after the cancer was diagnosed, and never again had a problem with her ulcer. She was a seasoned afghan maker. I treasure the one she gave me not long before she died as a thank-you for my refusal to let her die that one night.

I feel a bit uncomfortable telling that story, because I believe so strongly in people deciding what is best for them, even when it is fear that keeps them from getting care they need. Though I feel frustrated and inadequate, even sad, when I have not successfully worked with someone to get past fear, I don't usually jump in and take over. With Roberta that night, I gambled. Did I step over a line that defines the boundary between doctor and patient? I guess I judge myself partially guilty of that. It was her decision, but I inserted myself into it, which felt both personal and professional. On the other hand, because my action, albeit verbal, was dramatic, it probably influenced Roberta's decision to go to the ER.

I think of her when the topic of boundaries comes up. Our relationship reminds me to stop and think about how we and others place limits on any of our relationships, to question whether, at any given moment, the line is drawn in the best place, and at times to have the courage to move it closer or further and to cross it.

Doctors work within boundaries all the time. Many forces, professionalism, time, personal style and culture, self-protection, and the culture of medicine, shape these. They may vary some for different specialties and locations; a rural doctor will have closer ties with patients outside of the office, while urban doctors can maintain greater distance. There is also fluidity. Sometimes maintaining tight boundaries provides the environment where patient and doctor can work best. With others we can be looser. Often we really do not know what will work.

Boundaries are also universal, playing a role in shaping each of our relationships, in what we share with our bus driver, family members, best friends, checker at the supermarket. The tension for health care providers and patients exists because often our best care is not just predicated on the technical; it involves a connection between physician and patient.

Defining Limits
Anonymous

I met George about eight years ago. He is now close to 80 and has heart disease. He had one heart valve repaired and has to take blood thinners, which he does not like. He also does not like his inability to exercise as he could in the past—his heart just won't let him. For years I tried to help him understand the complexity of his medical condition and why he doesn't feel as well as he would like, but he did not accept my explanations. He just continued to complain. He was referred to me by another patient, who has since apologized to me repeatedly for doing so. Initially I would respond to these apologies with "Oh, that's fine, don't worry about it," all the while thinking, "Oh, please don't send me any more like George."

Every visit had a similar pattern, George telling me he did not feel well and me trying to help him understand why, while also trying to adjust his medications. He would inevitably launch into complaints about his interactions with other doctors, leaving me really uncomfortable. There was the doctor who arrived a half-hour late for a visit with him and never apologized, or the heart surgeon who entered with his entourage "like he was a king or something."

In the next breath, though, he would be saying the same heart surgeon told him that his heart was "perfect" after valve repair. "Therefore," he reasoned with me, "my current symptoms can't be related to my heart. Why am I taking all these heart medications since my heart is perfect?" All of our visits had this repetitive back and forth—his criticizing other doctors while at the same time quoting them to counter my advice.

When I would try to end the visit that had already gone way over our allotted time, his anger would flare "Don't tell me I need medicines," he would shout. "Dr. S told me my heart is perfect, and he's the chairman of his department."

I thought George wanted a "fix" to his problem and that my job was to help him understand there wasn't one. He was never going to feel as he had twenty years ago. His strength was weakened by a stroke and his heart, with his congestive heart failure, was no longer a strong pump. But as his voice rose, I would eventually back down, withdraw, and stop trying to explain. The visit would end and at the next visit, the conversation would repeat.

A few months ago I responded to George's complaints by expressing my own frustration. "Maybe you don't trust me or believe me? I think you're frustrated, and I know I am. If you don't feel like you can believe me or trust me, maybe you would like to find a different physician, one you can trust."

He became quiet, which was extremely unusual for him.

"You should think about this and we can talk about it next time," I said, ending the encounter. I wasn't sure I would see him again, but I noticed that my words silenced him, making the closure on the visit easier than it ever had been. At the time, I felt kind of a catharsis telling him that if he didn't trust my advice or me, he might do well to find a new doctor. I was trying to set limits with him by telling him how I felt. But my catharsis was accompanied by a little guilt. What happens with my patients should not be about me. At the same time, if he did not get value in our encounters, why were we having them?

Surprisingly, he did return after four months for his regular appointment. He tearfully recounted, "I was devastated when you told me to find another doctor. I told my cardiologist and he said maybe you were just having a bad day."

I was surprised and told him, "No, I never told you that you needed to find a new doctor. I said you could if you don't trust me." But his comments hit me. Had I really been in a bad mood at the time? I had thought I was using my well-honed communication skills to set limits. And was I trying to set limits with him so he would hear my advice, or was I creating a protective shield for myself? In so doing, had I missed that there been more to our relationship than just my advice, which he always seemed to want to reject?

At that same visit, he told me he was taking medication for his urinary symptoms. I had failed for months to get him to try this medicine, but on first meeting with a nurse practitioner in urology, she was able to get him to try it. What was in their relationship that was not in ours? And what was the meaning in our relationship that had him coming back, even though he was upset with me? I felt guilty again. Had I been too hard on him? Now that he had opened up and let me see that my words really upset him, I realized he actually was getting something from our interactions.

Now he comes in almost every month, which speaks volumes. I still don't have a quick fix, but I can provide a place where he can vent his anger at not feeling well. I feel closer to him. So from my perspective our relationship improved. He may still give me a hard time, but he always wants a hug at the end of our appointment. It's sweet. He seems a bit calmer, too. He can unload his frustrations about his failing health. And I feel I have more credibility and can say, "this is not going to get better," and not dwell so much on explaining my position. Maybe he is hearing me a little better, or maybe that was not the point in the first place.

About the guilt: I wrestle with interactions where I set limits, in particular if the other person is strong-willed and does not agree. I want clear boundaries, but if I set limits, I don't want them to be just for my purposes. If the other person does not see value in them, then those limits may not be helpful to him or to me. It's hard for me to do something just for myself and believe that doing so won't hurt and might even benefit the other person. Can I ask to get my needs met with patients or with family and friends without feeling selfish and prideful? My relationship with George is one place I am working on it.

Clear Boundaries

Crystal Kong-Wong

Visit 1:

New patient to me. Chief complaint according to the schedule: she wants a referral. Running 40 minutes late in my schedule because she took up all my Medical Assistant's time. In the exam room I see a 50-something woman, dressed nicely, but looking older than she is. Her walker is by her side, and she has several shopping bags with her.

I open with, "Hi, I am Dr. Kong-Wong. What can I do for you today?"

She fidgets and jumps from topic to topic, telling me how awful another hospital was, something about her mother, abuse, and isn't it awful?

Pretty quickly I feel like the whole room is out of control.

Am I crazy? Why can't I keep the conversation on track?

Reviewed meds: fibromyalgia, on narcotics.

Ran it through my head: I do not prescribe narcotics for fibromyalgia.

Took a deep breath—patient already tearful, rambling. I finally stopped her and directly asked about fibromyalgia. She gets narcotics from her rheumatologist. I don't have to prescribe them.

Feeling relieved. It's not my problem. I'm always wary of patients like this asking me to prescribe medications I'm conflicted about. But now that I know she doesn't want narcotics, why is she here? Does she even need me as her primary care doctor? Ah, it boils down to the fact that she wants a referral to the orthopedic surgeons for a knee replacement.

OK, they will look into her X-ray history. Referral given.

My thoughts and emotions jumbled: angry, sad, grateful, and changing moment to moment.

Visit 2:

Patient here again. She wants new X-rays. She tells me the same stories: how doctors fail her, how the doctors at the other hospital tried to take her mother away from her, how only I can help her. I feel kind of rude interrupting her, but if I don't, we won't get anywhere.

One minute she is praising me, then she is tearful, then angry with me.

I order her X-rays. She wants a chest X-ray too. I don't think it's indicated. She went for knee X-rays and returned demanding the chest X-ray. I tell her I won't order it.

She leaves. I don't think I'll see her again. She seems to "split." Everything is black and white, all good or all bad. Some doctors are wonderful (such as her rheumatologist who gives her narcotics), some are terrible (the ones who don't give her what she "needs").

She also tries to get too personal. At every visit I hear about the doctors at the other hospital, always with a question at the end, asking for my agreement that she was wronged, that she was a victim.

She keeps trying to get me to relate to her as more than a patient, pushing right up against my boundaries. I feel invaded and manipulated. She seems to need some emotional something, but we just met.

Trying to draw me into her drama: she's probably borderline.

Visit 3:

Did she really come back to see me? Thought for sure I'd be on the list of bad doctors. Anyway, she got an appointment with orthopedics. She is hopeful that she will get to see Dr. L. She only wants the "best."

Am I wrong? Did my referral give her false encouragement?

I don't think she's a great candidate for knee replacement.

Visit 4:

Comes back to update me. Shows me an ulcer on her leg. It seems to be from venous stasis, where the veins in the legs become dilated and don't return blood to the heart as effectively as before.

She starts right in with the same story, telling the trauma of the events at the other hospital. She still wants me to agree with her. Tearful. Histrionic.

Same old, same old.

I want to take a medical history. The ulcer looks "OK" to me, but I can't get through to her. She won't answer questions, even to tell me about the ulcer. Again she complains about other doctors, tells me that I'm different, complains about the other hospital. Am I even doing anything for her?

Telephone message: Patient denied surgery request by Dr. L. Oh shit. Now she's going to have a breakdown. Is she on my schedule?

Visit 5:

Patient here. Was seen by an orthopedic surgeon at the other hospital and was accepted for surgery.

Really?

Then she says she lied to the surgeon to get approved, telling him she wasn't on narcotics or methadone.

She is tearful, afraid she would get turned away if he knew. Says she needs a pre-op physical. No time for this today.

I told her I had to be honest and would put an accurate medication list, as well as discuss her chronic pain, in her physical exam report to him. She says she wants to be honest; she feels guilty.

Will see patient back for physical. Still wondering if she'll turn on me one day.

I'm very conflicted about this patient. I don't "like" this patient *per se*, but by now I've seen her five times and have a relationship with her. I think she has irrational expectations of this surgery and I still don't think the knee replacement is going to be the magic therapy that fixes all her ills. Her lies to the surgeon to get this done add to my conflict.

How often do patients bend or obscure the truth with doctors? Obviously it wasn't my place to call this MD and spill the beans, but it also didn't feel ethical to just clear her for surgery without addressing her medications and problems. I wanted the surgeon to have a fair chance to decide whether or not she was a good candidate. I told her up front about this because I didn't want to be in conflict myself.

I was glad I had set boundaries with her. When she told me she had lied, I was not at all conflicted about what I would do. One of our faculty, reviewing the visit with me, remarked how I had managed and pointed out that this patient would be helped by clear boundaries. In my personal life, I tend to have fairly clear boundaries. Maybe knowing that about myself helps me to work effectively with patients like this woman.

Ms. G and Mom
Chad Abbott

Before I met her, Ms. G's 35-year story traversed countless physicians, tests, surgeries, and prescription medications for her chronic neck pain. I entered her story-in-progress and attempted to shift its course to the direction I felt it should go. It did not occur to me until I hit my breaking point that my difficulty in dealing with this patient was greatly influenced by my relationships with my mother and my late father.

From early childhood, I have been a caregiver. My father died in 1999, when I was 27 and I was his in-home caregiver for the last months of his life as a homebound, depressed, debilitated man. Presently I am called on to be the caretaker for my mother. It is hard for me to see the lines around what is mine, what is theirs, and what I can or cannot fix. Being Ms. G's doctor brought me face to face with the realization that my past enters into the pain and difficulty I have in setting up boundaries today.

When Ms. G and I met, I was a first year resident. She came for her first clinic visit with me, with uncombed brown hair and dressed in a big oversized sweater and sweat pants. Her shoulders rolled forward, her chin was on her chest, and she avoided eye contact, wiping tears often from her chronically inflamed eyes. She just generally looked like she was shrinking towards disappearing. I was her doctor for a year or so.

She came to see me for her chronic neck pain and was on a large dose of narcotic medication. In addition to the 30 years of chronic pain, her tears, posture, and downward glance suggested she was depressed, with a lot of personal psychological pain. She was not employed, and I'm not sure what her former occupation had been. I would have liked to know more about her, but we never seemed to be able to discuss anything except the pain medications and her fear and distrust of physicians.

What had started her pain? Sifting through her records did not yield helpful information, and trying to elicit the beginning of a 30-year-old saga from her was impossible. It was not on her agenda, and time did not permit. She did spend a lot of time telling me the names and medical disciplines of no fewer than ten physicians who had treated her over the years. They were from other communities and I didn't know them.

At one point, Ms. G confided that her father had verbally and physically abused her all through her childhood and apparently, he still verbally abused her in adulthood. She told a story about a day when they had an argument and he actually kicked her across a room. I don't have more details because at that point, and any time she would speak of her father, she broke down, sobbing uncontrollably and looking at the ground. That story explained a lot about her distrust of men, and of me as her doctor.

Our main struggle every month was the discussion of other treatments that would make it possible to decrease her narcotic pain meds. The amount of narcotic medication that she took monthly was the highest for any patient I cared for. I know now that every individual's perception of pain is subjective and depends on a multitude of factors, not just on the actual organic pathology. In this patient's case, I did not know what the organic pathology was and I suspected from early on that the emotional and psychological pain were at the heart of her issues.

Our residency gave us protocols and taught us management strategies for working with patients who take daily narcotics for chronic pain. My relationship with Ms. G required that I implement this teaching, including encouraging her to exercise, accept alternative treatments, and decrease narcotic use if at all possible. It did not go well.

At each visit, her husband accompanied her. Dressed casually in pressed khakis, a button-up shirt, spectacles, and nicely styled salt-and-pepper hair, he was a counterpoint to her appearance. He also was the verbally assertive one, requesting her medications and hovering like a father figure or protector for his wife. They had been married for more than fifteen years, and maybe because of the frequent physician changes, he too seemed distrustful of physicians and medicine. We never knew the back-story. At the first hint of introducing a plan to try other therapies or reduce her narcotics, he was the first to speak. "You are the tenth physician to take care of my wife. Why would you want to change the medications? I don't understand why you want to do this. I live with my wife. I see her in pain. I see her moaning."

"It sounds really hard for you," I might respond, hoping to engage him in how caring for her affected him.

He would usually pause and thank me for understanding, with "And that's why she needs her medications. It is all in the chart. Why can't you just do what others did and give her the pills?"

In one of our typical conversations he asked me to refer her to a surgeon, saying, "When the surgeon opens her up and they try to fix all the scarring, I want you there to see all that's wrong with her neck. Then you'll understand." And many times I heard, "You physicians don't listen. Why do we have to repeat the same story time and time again to every new physician? All we need are her medications, and it should not be so difficult. She needs every one of those pills to be able to do anything, to just get out of bed. I live with her pain."

The pattern of our encounters became predictable. The two main directions of our conversations depended on whether I would initiate a discussion about trying different approaches for her pain or simply refill her meds without any discussion. If I provided the medications, her husband would say I was the finest physician they had ever worked with. If I didn't, then he would routinely ask to see my attending (the supervising faculty doctor).

"Let's talk about exercise and stretching," I might suggest.

"Please go get your attending," would be his response.

"If we try adding an antidepressant and some counseling, it might help your pain, and then we might be able to decrease your narcotic medication."

"I want to talk with your attending," became his standard reply.

Residents discuss each encounter with an attending physician, or preceptor. The attending doctor does not, however, come to the exam room for every patient. Because of attendings' rotating schedules, it was rarely the same person two times in a row when I had visits with Ms. G, and physicians' narcotic-prescribing styles are as varied as physicians themselves. So many different approaches were suggested to me that it became very confusing. I felt like I was in the middle of the Bermuda Triangle, with my patient's husband on one side, the patient on another, and my attending on the third.

How was I going to care for this patient? "Best-laid plans" would be to have one attending from my team co-manage this patient with me for consistency and continuity. This did not happen. Each time the attending would come in or give me advice, the patient usually ended up with her medication, the dose unaltered, and no alternative strategies tried.

I hit my breaking point in a typical (for us) interaction. I wanted to reduce her medication dose a small amount. She sat with downcast eyes. Her husband asked to speak to my attending. I stood my ground. I thought it was wrong not to decrease her dose, and did not want to be part of continuing as before. Acknowledging our stalemate, I became quiet and said, "I wish you the best and I am sorry that we cannot work together, because I can no longer prescribe these medications for you." That was the day our relationship came to an abrupt end. If I would not prescribe narcotics, she would no longer be my patient; to get narcotics they would have to find a different doctor.

She looked up briefly, "Well, good luck with your career."

I actually went back to the preceptor room and cried. My rapport with that day's attending preceptor was not the best. He was unwilling to help me work with my emotions about this and just told me to calm down and document what I was willing to do. He reminded me we could not abandon the patient and was looking for information in her record to document why I was going to stop being her doctor. She was transferred to one of the faculty doctors in our practice, and I think ultimately left our clinic for yet another practice group. I felt frustrated, defeated, even a little angry that our interactions seemed all about them "winning" exactly what they wanted every time.

It has always been difficult for me to accept the things I can't change and to allow people to make their own stories, maintaining a clear sense of the line between us. In an effort to help, I have at times interrupted someone else's story with what I think should be happening or what they should be doing. My interventions don't usually fix the situation, and I end up feeling disillusioned and frustrated. This patient relationship brought my tendencies into sharp focus. As a result of what I see, I am motivated to work on setting appropriate boundaries, not just with future patients, but also with my mother, for the sake of all of us.

One Size Doesn't Fit All
Roger Rosenblatt

He was a professor at the university and a colleague. We bumped into each other at a social event many years ago, and he asked if I would become his physician. I said yes. The problems started pretty quickly—because of boundary issues. He was an aging warrior who tended to abuse his body by engaging in challenging but episodic athletic pursuits, and came to me with demanding expectations. I was supposed to fix him and do it rapidly.

Prior to email we were able to manage our relationship. He would make an appointment, come and see me, and we would work through his problems. When we got email, he was one of the first patients to use it. This was years before any etiquette about email and patient care had been worked out. He emailed me frequently, asking questions. It felt like a misuse of access to me. He also over-interpreted my responses and regularly tried to replace visits with emails. During one episode where he misinterpreted an email exchange and started using an over-the-counter medication rather than come in to see me, he actually put himself in danger. Telling him this, I suspended his email privileges. He kept emailing me anyway. After a few months of his refusal to tolerate the email ban, I told him I could no longer be his doctor, and "fired" him from my practice.

It was easier to set limits in the other place I've been a family doctor—on my little block here in town, and where we have our cabin. Those cases were usually very comfortable. People came to me and asked questions. Sometimes I talked as a doctor, but more often as an information source. When people asked me questions, I had a very low threshold for suggesting that they see their own physician. I made it very clear that I was not assuming responsibility for their medical care.

The only time I got into trouble was when I violated my own rules while trying to help out neighbors with whom I had become quite friendly. They had no health insurance, and there was a history of serious psychiatric illness and substance abuse in the family. To spare them the expense of an emergency room visit, I unwisely gave them prescriptions for things like antibiotics. They ended up way too dependent on me and I crossed way too far over prudent boundaries when their car was stolen and I loaned them the money to replace it.

The whole situation came to a head one night. After having too much to drink, the wife banged on my door in the middle of the night after a fight with her husband. My wife and I spent a couple of hours making sure no one was hurt, and finally got them to patch things up. The next day when the wife came over again, I said, "You need to stop drinking and get some counseling." They never spoke to me again and soon after this, they moved away.

I am a person who needs to have things pretty controlled, and am uncomfortable when boundaries blur. In these instances I felt anxious; it really got too confusing for me. Raised by an autocratic father, I've also always worked in a hierarchical system, both as a commissioned officer in the Public Health Service and at the university, which is relentlessly hierarchical. I have hopefully gotten clearer about boundaries throughout all my relationships over time, but I incurred a lot of wounds along the way.

There are some happy endings, though. I recently ran into a man working in a rural hospital near our family cabin. He remembered me and still tells the story of his son's birth more than twenty years earlier. He lived next to us, an hour from the hospital, where he and his wife had gone for their son's birth. The baby got a bit jaundiced, but the couple wanted to go home. Their doctor (a close friend of mine) told them they would have to come back in three days to be examined, but then he remembered that we were coming over for a ski weekend. He called me. "Bring your black bag. You're going to make a house call." I did and proclaimed the baby to be in vigorous, no longer jaundiced, good health. The baby is now an adult, and obviously this was a very important event in the life of this family.

I really like other people, am very gregarious, and like to feel needed and useful. I see my mission in life as relieving suffering, mitigating injustices, and tilting at windmills, which sometimes tilt back. I have had to learn to balance my control impulses with my desire to be helpful, and to draw the line carefully between taking on someone's medical care – in general I'm NOT their doctor – but still being supportive and helpful.

Amy Died

Sarah Hufbauer

She often wore black boots with bold carnival-striped stockings, short skirts, and arm-length gloves of black or stripes with the fingers cut out. Hand-painted purses, book covers, dog collars, cigarette box holders, and more were carried along on her daily journeys, those walkabouts with only a few points on the map pinned down for certain and the rest left up to chance and curiosity. She was so forgetful and distracted that she often left her handmade purses behind on buses or in parks. She lost her cigarettes, her medications, and her books—she loved to read classic Russian literature like Dostoevsky. *Anna Karenina* was one of her favorites. She also listened to National Public Radio endlessly whenever she had a working radio. She had a tattoo of three cocktail glasses on her thin wrist to remind her that three drinks was her limit.

Her name was Amy Died. She became my patient around 1998, when her previous physician retired. As colleagues, her doctor and I discussed this very difficult patient years before I met her. I had heard about Amy's self-destructive behaviors along with her very strong constructive and creative forces. When she became my patient, I asked her what her name, Amy Died, meant. She told me that the original Amy was already dead, that she had faced thoughts of death and suicide so often that it was as if it had already happened. With this name the current Amy, the artist, could move on and be less hypnotized by that chasm between life and death. Putting her death into her name, and in the past tense, was also her brave gothic way of shocking people into grasping her struggles.

Amy gathered wood scraps from all over the city and then, with power tools, shaped them into amazing sculptural works of art. She came to clinic regularly to get her ongoing pain medications for her severe arthritis in her lower spine. Even by her late thirties, she'd take a Percocet tablet and then get in two to three hours of heavy-duty sculpting. Her previous physician and later I, too, believed we were enhancing her function and quality of life by prescribing opiates. Unfortunately, as she became more tolerant, it took ever-increasing doses to get the same benefit.

Despite this, I was relieved and gratified to visit one of Amy's successful shows in a gallery in 1998, the first year I started caring for her. I was amazed at Amy's bold strong work. Not necessarily beautiful, her often rough-hewn pieces had a certain grace in their edges and curves. She had to dumpster dive and scavenge to get many of the vintage wooden scraps she used, and she did this despite her back and neck pain, despite her mental health challenges and alcohol use.

When she came into clinic, she always had Molly, her beautiful Irish setter companion dog, at her side, often with a colorful kerchief and her hand-painted collar around her neck. At times Amy's other companion was her husband, a sweet blond man named Mark who kept her somewhat functional. When Mark left her, Amy tried to commit suicide several times, but only when she found someone to take care of her beloved Molly. She tried again after Molly died at age 12. She attempted an overdose at least twice. She jumped off a building once. After ingesting a multitude of pills, she always called someone, or 9-1-1, before falling asleep so that the act would not be final. She was apologetic each time at her next clinic visit, especially when the attempt was with an overdose; she knew I would feel responsible. She knew I was married with a two small children. In 2002 she gave me a sculpture that remains in our bedroom. It's almost six feet tall, a woman holding a toddler in one arm and with another child standing at her hip. At the base on the woman's foot is written "Doctor Sarah" in indelible ink. The piece is striking: arms and legs jut out, but with softness and curves around the breast and hip. The torso of the toddler, my son, is a lengthwise half of a violin. I can't remember how I got it from the clinic to my house. I paid her $200 in July of 2003, transforming it from a gift to a purchase when she needed the cash. As Amy's health declined, she got around less, and her many sculptures were put in storage and then sold when she couldn't pay her rent. Who knows if these strange and beautiful pieces just ended up in a dumpster again, from whence they came before she connected the pieces into something strong and beautiful? From wreckage to unique image to wreckage once more. Her chaotic and abusive childhood was the wreckage from which she built an artistic existence, but it all crumbled again into chaos as she became homeless and alone.

Though she had been a long-time smoker, we had no idea about her heart valve disease until she was fairly far into congestive heart failure. She had begun retaining fluid, and despite diuretics and consultations, it became clear that her congenital or acquired valvular dysfunction was neither operable nor treatable by medications alone.

She was hospitalized and although I spoke with her regularly on the phone when my colleagues were caring for her during that hospitalization, I visited her just once during her 20-day hospital stay. During that visit, she asked me for stronger pain medications and for initiation of hospice care. The medical team was moving in that direction, but they were ambivalent about making her sufficiently comfortable with opiates, knowing that she had sought narcotics all her life. I was only modestly helpful, also thinking that her desire for opiates was another somewhat unreasonable way for her to deal with her mostly emotional suffering. They didn't realize, nor did I, that these would be her last days.

She also had let us know that she did not want to be alone or in pain when she was dying. Those wishes were not granted by the hospital team, who tried to find balance and restraint in their care for Amy and who did not realize her imminent death. When I visited her, I also did not perceive the urgency of her requests, and when a friend of hers arrived to see her, I made a hasty retreat, saying a goodbye that in no way honored our ten-year relationship.

There was no time to notify me when she went into cardiac arrest, and she died without loved ones nearby. She had let us know she did not want to be resuscitated, and her wishes were respected. Amy died at 10 AM on August 15, 2008 from heart failure with respiratory distress. She was 49.

If I had really been present to see and hear Amy's pain and fear at the end I would have been sure to get her the end-of-life opiates and comfort she needed. I would not have walked out, leaving it to other doctors who hardly knew her.

My desire to avoid being co-dependent prevented me from being as fully compassionate with Amy as I would have liked. While I had become one of the closest people she had in her life toward the end, she was clearly less than that to me. Somehow I allowed that disproportionate and asymmetric need to push me back. While the power dynamic and hierarchy of physician and patient is usually apparent, sometimes it becomes more obstructive of good care, especially at end of life, than it needs to be.

In the end, when Amy died, I was not there emotionally or physically. Managing my busy outpatient clinic patients and getting home to my own family took priority over extra visits to the hospital to check on my sweet, brilliant, troublesome patient. The days had passed, and I didn't imagine the end of her life was approaching. She had bounced back from overdoses and traumatic falls so many times that I didn't imagine her actually taking her last breath there in the hospital.

I deeply regret not being there to give Amy comfort. During many of our office visits over the years, I reflected back to her that I saw in her the inner strength and resilience needed to meet and get through each day's suffering and loneliness. I wish I could have reminded her closer to her death that she could depart this life with the same grace. I wish I could have lessened her fear and loneliness. Perhaps this time she knew she could do this on her own. But I wish I could have told her how much her irreverence and individuality, which made her medical care so difficult, were also valuable to me as her physician—to learn from each visit and each phone call that I was not solely in charge. Her medical care and our therapeutic relationship were always a co-creation. From Amy's life and from her death I learned that pain can sometimes be transformed into strength and beauty. I learned that an odd and brashly clad persona often hides a hurting, scared person. I learned that my boundaries and pride keep some distance between my patients' suffering and me as a way of protecting myself from the pain in their lives. Yet sometimes a more vulnerable approach with defenses down might make a world of difference in someone's life (or dying).

I miss Amy greatly and wish I could have one last time to tell her how much I appreciate her sculpture in my room, and how her life was worthwhile, even though short and full of struggle. Seeing a recent Picasso exhibit, I tried to imagine her big smile, as if she could see how Picasso, too, made sculpture out of found objects, using art as a truth amidst the lies of life. Amy would have loved that shared experience. Having known and cared for Amy, I appreciate unusual artistic expression as a deeply personal sharing much more than previously. Even though our last time together was so brief, and regrettable for me, my world remains deeply enriched by Amy's existence and even by her pain.

Postscript

To get permission to use Amy's chosen last name, the author/editor of this book, Sharon Dobie, and I located and met with Amy's sister. As she read the story I wrote, her responses were matter of fact. She told us that she had been able to stay in touch with her sister intermittently throughout the years. They would meet at a donut shop downtown when she had a work meeting in the area and Amy often asked her sister to give her money. During Amy's last stay at the hospital before her death, and unbeknownst to me, her sister visited her several times weekly. She shared that she was there when Amy had predicted her death the day before it happened. She also viewed their childhood very differently than Amy's frequent rants about the abuse she suffered. Clearly their life stories had very contrasting arcs.

Meeting with Amy's sister brought me the gift of great relief—knowing that she was at Amy's bedside the day before Amy died and that Amy was not as alone or abandoned as I had thought. I am grateful for Amy's sister's generosity of time and sharing.

Finding the Balance
Sharon Dobie

Helen was a short, stocky redhead going gray. I can't remember how she became my patient, but she seemed angry with me from the day we met. She had fired several doctors, including specialists. She proudly told me, "They tried to get me to do this and that, harrumph!" And she never finished the sentence.

Over the first three years she was my patient, I could not figure out why I was her doctor. She took her blood pressure medications, but she only intermittently took her medications for her asthma and chronic lung disease (emphysema). During most visits with me, she would spend a good portion of our time on long soliloquies about my inadequacy. "I don't know why you're giving me that medicine. It does NOT work. The specialists say I should take it, too, but what do they know? Do any of you know what you're doing?" I never witnessed her interactions with staff, but they frequently asked me why she was so angry.

I couldn't figure it out. I'd ask questions, but she would never tell me much about her personal life. She was in her early 70s, lived alone in her own home, was retired from an office job, and told me she had one really good friend, a man in his 50s.

"He doesn't have any friends. He has some sort of emotional trouble and is sad. He helps me around the house and then we sit at the kitchen table and talk. Well, I talk. He never says much, but seems to enjoy having some company."

About twice a year she would have a flare of asthma and be hospitalized. We would again revisit the factors that contributed to her health and illness. And then she would again get angry with me, telling me to stop telling her what to do.

As she aged, I became increasingly concerned that there might be a lot of dust in her home. I wondered if she needed help with housecleaning, but she declined any assistance. Actually, our clinic nurse and I suspected she was hoarding. Most of our older patients will let us visit them at home, because it saves them a trip to the clinic, is social, and allows us to help them evaluate the safety of their home. Helen repeatedly refused. Her hospitalizations continued, she continued to take her medications only sporadically, and she continued to be angry with me. When she checked in at our clinic, she would tell the staff that she wanted more visits with the specialists she saw for her emphysema, asthma, and heart disease, but she never made more appointments with them, even though she could have done so. Instead, she came to see me, even though she never seemed to be content with me as her physician.

I would steel myself for her visits, expecting a barrage of comments about how unhelpful I was and how she really needed to be in the primary care of a pulmonologist or cardiologist. Maybe she was just fearful and didn't trust me, or any doctor. Maybe she used her anger as a way to keep me at a distance where I could not get to know her better. I was never able to actually clarify our conflict. As our interactions settled into a predictable pattern, I felt that her inability or unwillingness to manage her anger or change providers was disrespectful and unhealthy for both of us.

After two years of pacing back and forth to calm myself before each of her visits, I decided it was enough. If I was so inadequate, she could – and should – get another doctor. But I was afraid of setting limits with her, perhaps because I did not want to upset her. Since she had not sought a different doctor and had fired several, I worried that her reaction would be to stop seeing anyone and stop her medication. And I don't like to let people down. Still, after a few more visits with her, I believed she should get a new doctor. I talked with our clinic manager, and then I met with Helen.

"Helen, I would like to talk about your health care and who should be your primary care doctor," I opened. "At most of our visits you seem upset with me, often downright angry. Clearly, I'm not meeting your needs. It can't be healthy for you to have so much dissatisfaction, and it's unhealthy for me to be constantly criticized about things that are not going to change."

"Well, I've told you, I don't think you're helping me. I should be followed by the pulmonary doctors or cardiologists."

"They recommend seeing you once a year in follow-up, and I have always said you can schedule with them more regularly if that's what you want. That is up to you, not me. I still believe you will benefit from a primary care doctor who knows you. I'm not sure why you come to see me, but at this point I want to discuss finding you a new doctor, one who can meet your needs better than I have."

"What? Are you trying to get rid of me?"

"No, I want to work with you to find a physician with whom you can work and not feel so angry and dissatisfied all the time. I have some ideas and finding this person will be better for your health and mine."

"No! Absolutely not. I'm not changing doctors. I almost have you trained," she said, close to tears.

And then we both laughed at the clarity of that statement.

Once I could stop sputtering, I told her I would reconsider my decision. "I cannot continue to work with you unless there are some changes," I told her. We then had a discussion about her behavior during visits. I clarified that having me trained did not include the right to attack me at every visit. We talked about how she treated staff; I told her that a bottom line for me was that she treat the clinic staff with respect. We discussed her rights and responsibilities to choose another doctor, see the specialists more often, and to choose to work with me in a more congenial way.

After that, we worked fairly well together, and I continued to be her doctor until her death five years later. She still would come in complaining that there was no point in medications and that she would prefer visits with specialists, but she stopped the yelling, the rancor was gone, and staff reported that she was polite. She remained cantankerous until the end, never letting us see her house, resisting the move to assisted living, and complaining about the food and conditions after her move to that facility. Yet she and I had come to an agreement, reinforcing for me the truth that setting some limits can be healthy for all and does not have to end with disaster.

There are also times when we stretch the boundaries. During residency, I cared for a 65-year-old man who, while visiting our city, had a devastating stroke. He was found unconscious in a hotel downtown and brought by the medics to the county hospital where I worked. He had no identification on him. When he regained consciousness, he had right-sided weakness, and his attempts to communicate with us came out as gibberish. He couldn't write, either. This is called an expressive aphasia and is typical of the kind of stroke that he had. The problem was that he couldn't tell us who he was, where he came from, or what had happened in the hours leading up to his stroke.

His gestures and facial expressions told us he was upset. But only after several days could we tell that he could understand some of what we were saying, suggesting that the part of the brain that receives information was working fine. His gibberish speech was rapid-fire, with a tempo more fast-paced than our neurology colleagues had seen in patients after this kind of stroke. That did not help us sort out whom to call so this man could be reconnected to his prior world.

The police, working with the information he gave when checking into the hotel, found his family on the East Coast. We were able to piece together a version of his story. This man was single, had siblings and nieces and nephews, and had bipolar illness. He had stopped his medication, became manic, and flew to our city with no identification and hardly any luggage. He had the stroke in his hotel room.

After several weeks of rehabilitation at the hospital, he was stable enough to travel back home by plane. He could walk and had fairly good use of his right arm. His speech was still problematic, but he could say a few basic phrases. But there was no way to get him to the airport. Our hospital would not allow a cab, and he did not qualify for any other kind of escorted transportation. After some hair pulling and team discussions, another resident and I put him in my Volkswagen bug, drove him to the airport, escorted him to the gate, and ensured he boarded the plane home.

There are some black and white boundaries in the patient-doctor relationship, just as there are in all relationships. There is also a lot of undefined territory where each of us faces choices about where to draw the boundary line and where to stand in relation to that line. The practice and the challenges of this aspect of doctoring can, for many of us, be the training ground for improving other relationships in our lives. Regardless of where we are on the spectrum, from having trouble setting limits, to having overly rigid boundaries, what we see in our clinical practice can shed light on what we see in our personal behavior. In our relationships, how are our boundaries decided?

Chapter 8

Bias, Assumption, and Learning Tolerance

The stories in the next three chapters consider some related questions. In this chapter, the authors tell stories about encounters where they faced their own assumptions, biases, and judgments and in some cases made progress towards understanding and changing. Chapter 9 authors ask how well we can really know another, whether those limits stem from barriers and boundaries imposed upon us, from those that we create, or simply as a consequence of our human reality. Authors in Chapter 10 notice those relationships where the patient unknowingly is a mirror for the physician, prompting self-understanding.

Whining—Was It?
Sharon Dobie

We all have patients who grate on us. Darryl was a guarantee for me.

Before seeing him, I would clutch the counter outside the exam room and take a few deep breaths, talking to myself. "You can do this. You can be cheerful. You don't need to be derailed by him." Certain he would be wanting more pain medication and would not have kept his end of the bargain, going to physical therapy, I would enter the his exam room.

As soon as I saw him, I would have to pull out another technique: deflection? reflection? I would picture myself holding a big reflecting shield in front of me. All the darkness, dejection, and anxiety would not enter me, but would instead be reflected back to him, where it had anyway originated, leaving me able to be there and hear him, though unsure I could help him.

There Darryl would be: sitting in the chair by the desk, maybe in those ridiculous blue paper shorts we give patients whose legs we need to examine. The shorts can fit anyone between 100 and 300 pounds, as long as the 100-pounder has a belt to hold them up. Or maybe Darryl would be fully clothed—in faded jeans and sweater (winter) or T-shirt (summer, if we were having a summer). His hair was always a bit disheveled, in need of trimming. Usually he would look up at me, sometimes avoiding eye contact. Was he really waif-like or just a good actor?

"Well, hi! It's nice to see you. What brings you in today?" – my standard opener. Ball is in your court, Darryl.

Deep sigh. "Doc, the pain is just not getting any better." – his standard reply.

By the time I first met him, a good year before this encounter, he was in his 40s and had been through a lot of living. An active IV-drug user and alcoholic, he had achieved brief periods of sobriety in his early 30s. He had a child, now grown, who was doing well, and I was never sure who had raised her. After community-college training during one of his clean and sober periods he got a job as a construction worker, and then had a fall. He lived, and luckily his brain was fine afterward, but his knee and hip were badly fractured. When we met, he believed the initial surgeries had been botched because he had been uninsured at the time. He was not much more satisfied with a subsequent revision that apparently did little to give him more mobility and less pain.

In my care, we had put him on a pain contract and some ongoing narcotic medication, pending a second revision surgery, which had been scheduled when we first met. The pain contract is a contract signed by patient and doctor. The document reviews the risks of narcotics along with the benefits. There are a number of terms in the contract: a patient agrees to take only what is prescribed, to only get prescriptions from the primary doctor, to fill the prescriptions at the same pharmacy, not to get narcotic meds anywhere else, and to understand that losing them, having them stolen, or taking extra will not result in an earlier refill.

Darryl came up short one month and asked for an early refill. Not quite the "dog ate them" excuse, but it was close, yet believable: "My cousin, who is an addict, got into them and stole them." Family members seemed to think this was plausible, so we gave him one exception and refilled his medication. Within two months, he violated the contract by going to an ER and getting narcotics there, rather than telling them he was on a contract and could only get them from me. We stopped prescribing.

He went on to have a second revision surgery that necessitated post-operative narcotic medication. He, his orthopedic surgeon, and I formed an agreement that I (and my clinic) would manage his post-operative outpatient pain and medication prescribing. I have done this for 8-10 patients over the years who needed surgery and post-operative narcotics, and who were also addicts in recovery and therefore at high risk for relapse. We all signed another contract. As is commonly done in these situations, he and his family agreed that they would store and distribute his narcotics to him based on the schedule we gave him.

So here he is: sad eyes, constant pain, immobility, and today wanting help, having arrived ten minutes late for his fifteen-minute appointment. I resolved to smile, try really hard to hear him, and search for ways to help him handle pain, live with pain, and keep moving with pain. This is what he needs to do and that is what I promote. And I am sure he has not done the physical therapy that will ultimately help him.

"How's PT? Are you going?"

"It's hard to get a ride. I went twice and honestly, it didn't help. I hurt too much to do anything," he crescendoes into a good whine. I am sure what his next lines will be and hopefully my mood will not soon mirror his.

"I…"

What now? What can I possibly offer him? He had the definitive surgery. Rehabilitating it will take time—and work. He wants no pain—now. "Darryl," I try again before he can go on. "You had surgery. You're on adequate medication to minimize your pain. Your leg has been through a lot. Shoot, *you* have been through a lot. Look, this is going to take hard work. We talked about this before you had the last surgery, how no one could do the rehab but you. Where are you on this?"

"Hey! Let me finish. You don't care that I'm tired. I want my life back. I want to go to school and get a job."

"I know. We're talking about now, the next two weeks, the next two months, what you need in order to be able to do the work, in order to do the work. What will it take? No med will answer that. It's your work that your leg needs."

I can feel my patience draining. Our 15-minute visit was over ten minutes ago and I have two patients waiting. But the issue is bigger than his leg. His healing is complicated by past pains, by the addiction, and by all that has gone wrong in his life. Though we had long discussions about this, both before and after his surgery, he does not seem to connect the relationship of all these factors with his pain. Fear that he wants me to take on the responsibility for all of it overwhelms me in the now oxygen-deprived space where we sit. So I just look at him.

Expecting to next see eyes stare at the floor and shoulders slump with stubborn resistance, what comes next is a surprise.

"No one understands. Why don't you listen to me? You just want me off the drugs. Everyone does. You all think a surgery and physical therapy appointments will fix it all. You think it's my fault that I need the pain meds. So ya know it is not so simple. After those first two times, I said, 'no more.' Then my sister called and agreed to drive me and gave me a pep talk. So I started up again and I've been four more times, and I need the meds still, but maybe it's helping, the PT stuff. They said maybe try massage too, but it's not covered. I can't afford it."

There I was, caught red-handed, finishing his sentence with my assumptions. He left with a prescription in his hand, to fulfill another pain contract requirement and leave a urine sample for toxicology/drug screen. I left the room feeling bedraggled, judged, and judging.

Later that day, writing up notes from the day's visits, I recognized that haggard feeling I sometimes have after a challenging clinic. It clearly came from the visit with Darryl. I don't trust him; I'm biased towards not believing him. Worse, I'm put off and irritated by what I perceive to be complaining and a lack of personal initiative. I had approached him assuming he had not done physical therapy or the exercises that will ultimately help his pain to lessen. I entered the room guarded, steeled in case (I assumed) he wanted more than the agreed-to amount of pain medication. But he had gone to PT and he did not ask for an increase in his narcotic dose.

He doesn't trust me, or any doctor. Probably this predates his earlier addictions and his fall and broken bones, but those experiences also seem to have fed his bias, his vulnerabilities. I didn't help reverse those feelings that day with my own! And I wonder if he knows that his tossing out the "You don't care" unsettles me and would unsettle many doctors.

I don't like to have preconceived notions. I much prefer being tolerant and curious. At times I am neither, and it's not just in my clinical work.

One bias of mine that shows up working with Darryl is about complainers. My internal voice: "Why not just get on with it and do something about it? Accept it, change it, or leave." How often am I the guilty party? Do I complain too much to my friends about this, that, or the other thing: work, life, whatever is on my mind?

While each of us has pretty predictable patterns of response, there's always the capacity for a different expression. And just because we might assume how a person will behave, based on what we know about that person, it does not mean that the behavior will be consistent with our predictions. With patients, sometimes stepping back from our biases and assumptions can lead to a better connection and to interventions that facilitate their care. And sometimes recognizing our biases leads us to take important personal inventory. The stories in this chapter are liberally dosed with humility, showing the opportunity for increasing both self-awareness and tolerance.

The Prodigal Son's Brother

Casey Law

I have a patient who pushes my buttons. She's an early 30-something blonde, engaged to be married, with a chubby one-year-old daughter. Alas, she also has a problem—actually, multiple problems—and I cringe when her name appears on my schedule. She has Hepatitis C and a lengthy history of poly-substance abuse including IV heroin. Oh, and she has Borderline Personality Disorder.

Caring for her, what have I learned about myself?

Perhaps I have not "learned" as much as awakened to the realization that deep down I harbor a glaring personal defect: I'll call it Unjustified Righteous Anger Complex (or "URAC" for short). For those who are biblical, this is also known as the Prodigal Son's Brother Syndrome. When the prodigal son returned home destitute and starving, having spent his inheritance in "riotous living," his staid and dependable brother became angry and resentful. ("You never threw me a party, dad!") Not much is known of this condition besides that it appears in all socio-economic classes, is gender-neutral, and is found in every ethnic group.

To make a diagnosis of URAC, at least three of the following diagnostic criteria must be met:

1) An unassailable and even smug sense of one's own piety;

2) Indignation at another's lack of piety;

3) Passive-aggressive displays of aforementioned indignation, at times accompanied by emotional outbursts;

4) In dealings with the object of indignation, a placid and even congenial outward appearance while secretly fuming with negative internal emotion; and

5) A tendency to critique the object of indignation, often while not in their presence.

Sadly, there is no cure. It can, however be successfully managed with appropriate treatment.

"Hello, my name is Casey."

"Hello, Casey."

"I have URAC."

There it is, I admitted it, and that's the first step: realizing I harbored intensely negative feelings toward someone who had done me no personal harm, was no worse a person than I, yet I felt justified in judging her as unworthy of my time or respect, and in front of whom I maintained a professional, all-smiles demeanor.

I'm getting better. You should have seen me back in the day, when I was way worse. Now my URAC is a much easier thing to handle, even though whenever it's brought to my conscious awareness, it makes me sad. Interacting with my blonde patient makes me sad. Yes, sad that she made poor decisions or was put in a position where she became addicted to drugs. Sad for her infant daughter's future. Sad for society. I feel helpless, too, shouldering the world's troubles, and for what? I can't do anything about who she is—who I am. Wait, can't I do anything about who I am? Yeah, I think I can, by trying to suppress the URAC. This comes with a gift.

Every few months, whenever she appears on my clinic schedule, I am forced to reevaluate my progress of becoming less judgmental, less holier-than-thou. This forced introspection is my therapy. I'm less judgmental of my friends, new acquaintances, and family members, and ultimately less judgmental and more forgiving of myself. She gives me this gift with every visit. And afterwards, at the end of the day, I get to unwrap it and contemplate a bit, and—I feel better.

Not Drowning

Anonymous

I sighed whenever she brought the children, usually the two youngest ones. Toys all over the exam room, the two kids competing with me to attract their mother's attention, normal sibling fights leaving one of them crying. Or, when my patient was crying, the older one crawling into her lap with tears in his eyes and a pained, concerned expression, asking her if she was okay. There was always so much in her life story that had occurred since the last visit. The presence of the children smothered my last bit of a chance to absorb and make sense of at least some of what was going on. I felt lost in a chaotic ocean, drowned among the stories she was conveying to me, the simultaneous scenes in the exam room, and my beliefs about it all.

There was the son in Afghanistan. The other son with "puberty issues." Enormous marital distress. My patient's over-boiling anxiety and fear alternating with anger against everyone in her life story, including me, and then back to tears. Mood swings between helplessness, requests for help, and anger, back and forth. I was sinking further, the children distracting me, making me lose the story's threads.

And then there was the pain. Pain all over. She quoted her mother as saying, "You need to tell the doctor to give you more pain medicines." She quoted her husband, her sister. Everybody was apparently letting me know that she needed more narcotics to numb her. But the pain was deeper. Though I felt her pain, I could not reach it in the ocean of her emotion and fear. Neither could the pain medicines.

But my patient's interactions with her children struck me. In the midst of the immense chaos of her life and highly emotional encounters with me, she was calm, loving, and skillfully strict with her children. "No, your toys do not belong in the garbage bin," she quietly admonished one. He smiled, obeyed, and turned around and kept playing. "This is a very nice drawing you made, but I am talking with the doctor now and need you to play a little bit longer." All calm, focused, and clear.

Seeing this core of her being as a mother helped me resurface from chaos, to see the story, the thread, and recognize the core human nature that connects us, regardless of how much turmoil muddles our interactions. Too often we miss those cues because we get so carried away by difficult surface interactions that we don't notice the human core behind it all.

Her impressive parenting skills shone with her ability to connect skillfully with her children, leaving me humble and putting into perspective all the minor chaos I might experience in my life. Telling her what a wonderful mother she was gave me an honest connection with her. Stepping back and realizing all this gave me strength for the next encounter with her—maybe drowning, but a little less so.

Getting to Know Her

Genevieve Pagalilauan

Just reading her chart set me on edge, that day when I first went to see her. I was a first-year resident and she was on my schedule in my "continuity clinic," the one half-day I spent in my outpatient clinic during that first year. From her chart I could tell she was on four or five different narcotic and semi-narcotic medications plus benzodiazepines (anxiety medications). She had already had a gastric bypass and multiple hospitalizations for small bowel obstructions, and despite hypertension, high cholesterol, and coronary artery disease with angina, she was still smoking.

When I entered the room, I saw a heavyset, neatly groomed Caucasian woman in her late fifties. She smelled of tobacco. She had a long list of symptoms. She was falling more often and had pain in her back and knees. Her ongoing respiratory problems included shortness of breath and a cough, and she had frequent chest pain, acid reflux, abdominal pain, and constipation. She vomited if she ate even a little more than usual. Her liver tests were abnormal. So many symptoms! And she wanted her pain medications, all of them, refilled.

Instantly, I felt ill-equipped and ineffective. I tried to address her symptoms and at the same time knew I would need to change her narcotic regimen. Like others of my patients that year who came to me as new patients, bringing their histories and medication lists, she was wedded to her particular regimen. The science of what I had to say did not impress her.

In subsequent visits, she did not agree with me when I aggressively started trying to switch and consolidate her medications. It became clear we did not have a relationship as a basis for that work, and initially I did not get very far. She was upset with me, and I dreaded seeing her and then felt guilty about it. I used to have to say a peace mantra to calm myself prior to our visits, knowing that our discussions about medication had been contentious and uncomfortable for me. Early in our relationship, when I would recommend changes in her narcotic regimen, her response was, "You don't know what I need, and others started them for a reason. Why was I started if there wasn't a reason?"

Her appointments were monthly and usually opened with her long list of symptoms. I did not make headway until slowly, over time, I got to know her and what she valued in her life. Her pain might have been worse when she went to play Bingo, but it was an activity she enjoyed. She wanted to go on little family vacations with her children and grandchildren or to feel well enough to be in the back yard watching them play.

Directing our focus away from whatever the dominant symptom was, I could point out how the narcotic and anxiety medications actually might have contributed to a diminished quality of life. Maybe she would have less vomiting, constipation, and abdominal pain if she took fewer narcotics. Maybe she would be more alert to help care for her grandchildren. Maybe some of the pain would be tolerable if she were doing the things she loved.

When I started to listen to her, she started to listen to me. As we sorted through the medical issues, she stayed out of the hospital and became more active in her life. She talked about various family members with whom she lived; she talked about being a mom and pain she felt when she did not agree with how her kids raised their children. Showing me the baby's picture, she shared her distress that her daughter did not trust her to hold the newest grandchild. And we got her to a stable dose of one narcotic, with fewer intestinal side effects and fewer falls.

When I saw her mainly as someone who needed narcotics, we were on opposite sides of the issue of her pain medications and our conversations were adversarial. Once I knew her and got past my biases, she knew I cared, even if she did not agree with my recommendations. When I knew what she wanted to accomplish, it became easier to work together to mutually form plans for improving her health. I looked forward to seeing her and enjoyed our sharing of our lives. She saw me get larger with pregnancy, knew about my child, and gave grandmotherly advice about my second pregnancy.

A few years ago she was found unresponsive by family members, and died. I was on maternity leave at the time and I cried harder and longer for her than I was capable of crying for some of my own family members who had passed away.

Now that my practice is full, I unabashedly "cherry pick" my patients. Will I ever be the same person who so persistently worked through the biases sparked by all that I feared in my patient's chart to receive the gift of a relationship with her? What was it in our original tensions and struggles that facilitated for me this initially reluctant but powerful relationship? Have I formulated as deep a bond with my other patients? Perhaps it's the patients who expose our vulnerabilities and whose health acuity is more perilous that become our most cherished, maybe because they enable a frequency of exposure and create mutual reliance that builds mutual trust in an uncertain future.

She was my first patient who showed me the value of a doctor-patient relationship over time, that if we work as a team, we can accomplish a lot. The timing of our meeting and my novice status served us both well. As a new doctor, I over-explained everything and was too rooted in the science of medicine. She was unabashedly honest with me about the rigidity of some of my recommendations. Rather than pretend to agree and then go out and not follow them, she would say, "I do not agree. It won't work for me." I had to trust her, hear in honesty how was I coming off, and how was I perceived. And she was patient about letting a doctor-in-training work with her. Early on she must have made a judgment that I was trying hard and she was going to try with me. She watched and helped me grow.

She taught me about judgment as well. We all carry biases. We see someone for a split second and make a judgment based on what we see or hear: dress, size, skin color, habits. Getting to know her reminded me that each person has a life and struggles. When those snap assessments of persons cross my mind, they remind me of the shortcoming of being judgmental, both in my work and in my life outside of work. She provided me an opportunity to grow as a person, a more patient, more open person. Walking beside her on her journey gave shape to my instincts, values, and interests.

A Broader View

Ahalya Joisha

Mr. J is a man in his late 60s, one of the first patients I saw as a resident. He has bilateral hip and knee osteoarthritis and was living alone, on a Nutrisystem diet, hoping to lose weight for a planned hip replacement surgery. He had labile blood pressure and chronic pain issues as well as an enlarged prostate for which he consulted a urologist. In his younger days he had been an active volleyball player and a coach, and now it was difficult for him even to walk around. Because of his disabilities he had to change jobs and give up what he loved the most. When I met him, he was working in a book store. A friendly man, he was easy to get to know.

Over the first several months and multiple visits, I became fiercely protective of and responsible for him. For example, I did not take a sick leave one clinic day when he booked an appointment with me. Another provider might not meet all his needs; I knew him better. Besides his medical needs, I knew his social situation; I knew how sensitive and polite he was and that he might not express disagreement or bring up his problems with a new doctor. There were also some seemingly small issues that needed to be discussed (but which made a world of difference for him), like how to acquire a scale so that he could skip some office visits and weigh himself at home. Who could do these things better than I, his family doctor?

This case made me realize a few things about myself. I feel really responsible for my patients. I also realized that I enjoyed working with older individuals and helping them meet their medical needs as well as helping them live successfully and thrive in the community. And there was so much I did not know.

He opened my eyes to a broader world and to challenges I never would have known existed. About showering, for example. Mr. J would go days without showering because he could not get into his bathroom—his wheelchair would not fit through the door. Being able to shower was something I took for granted. Listening to his stories I realized how much I assume about how our patients cope. He gave me a glance into a life different from my own, a broader view.

Misreading
Sharon Dobie

Mr. P. had a backache. He was 67, African American, and a retired plumber with no good pension and no health insurance. He had used his back for his work life and at home doing upkeep on his aging house. When he came to see me with back pain, my exam did not reveal any reasons to be worried about anything worse than an arthritis flare. He was almost 70 and had other signs of arthritis, so that is how I treated him.

It seemed to be about the arthritis and the pain each time he came in. He was not interested in physical therapy or other ideas I had. Over four months, he got worse instead of better. Only in the fourth month did he reveal that he was not sleeping well and was awakening with worse pain. That worried me so I ordered an X-ray. There it was: one of his vertebrae looked like it had been chewed up. Further testing showed that he had multiple myeloma, a cancer that starts in cells in the bone marrow and often, if not found early, moves to bone. He underwent treatment for some months, but his disease was advanced when we found it and he died within a year.

He had come in looking like an older man with arthritis. Assessing him within that framework drew me away from a more inquiring stance that had a greater chance of unearthing the subtle. In this case, I'll never know if four months would have made a difference for him. But the outcome reminded me to quiet my first impressions and to be open to the subtle clues telling me that what is happening is sometimes not what seems obvious.

With family and friends, too, how often do I resist thinking I know what is going on or that I have the best grasp of the situation? How many of us go through life limiting our relationships by living personal fictions created by our assumptions and biases? Seeing beyond them makes greater insights possible in all of our relationships, allowing us to know others more deeply.

Chapter 9

Can I Really Know You? … Or Anyone?

I Thought I Knew You
Sharon Dobie

The exam room is uncannily quiet. I don't dare break the silence by typing in his chart. My hands are in my lap and I am facing him, waiting. His hair is over his eyes now, covering the adolescent acne on his barely stubbled face, but the shadow hiding his eyes is old. Did we fail this now 5'7", used-to-be-2'4" man-child who does not stand tall in self-esteem? Something in his self-told story told him that life may not be worth living. I thought I knew him, but did not see it coming.

My mind pans back to visits when Eric was three, four, five. He was in many ways a typical little boy, shy with me, yet never seeming afraid to come to see me. What story did he tell himself about his challenges during those years? When he was two, his dad was diagnosed with cancer and had a couple of years of chemotherapy, with everyone wondering if he would survive.

Eric came later than his sister to speaking and grasping a crayon to color. No one made a fuss about this, taking it pretty much in stride; his parents just signed him up for preschool, which was typical for kids his age. He had seemed to like that preschool. His mom told me she was happy to see him hopping from the car each morning and slow to leave each afternoon, and he was learning a lot. His articulation and skipping and crayon holding improved. Then came his tummy-aches. His colitis was elusive for years, and he spent those years in some pain, both physical and emotional, and on daily medication. But he did not seem unhappy. There were no signs that he was not adjusting to his challenges in a healthy way. Was there a piece that we didn't see?

As his doctor when he was in elementary school, did I miss that he was really trying to tell me he felt broken? When I would see him for ear infections or well-child exams, his mother would encourage him to tell me what was on his mind. Usually he was "ok," which translated to liked school, had friends, nothing to complain about. Over the years and not necessarily temporally close together, he admitted a couple of times to being sad, feeling like he was not as good as others. We would talk during those visits, try to dissect what saddened him. He was good at talking about the things he enjoyed and how he also just felt sad at times though he was unsure why. Based on our screening questions he never came close to the bar that would have raised major concern. But to be safe his parents had him do some work with a counselor. During our visits I would also share my feelings about how strong I felt him to be, handling the challenges he had, how smart he was in so many areas where he excelled in school.

I am sitting here facing him and his mom as she tells me calmly about the diary. They have found a good counselor, she tells me, but she wants me to know, in case. In case what?

"He is doing OK now. Right, Eric?" she looks furtively at her son, his eyes glued to the spot just beyond the toes of his Nikes. "What if things get bad again, and if he needed a psychiatrist or to be hospitalized?" she adds, reading my mind.

"Eric?" I keep looking at him hoping he might speak for himself. He'll shower when they ask him and maybe even bow to deodorant, yet he smells of adolescent sweat, sneakers, and sadness.

"I think I am better. And I won't hurt myself," is all he will offer to the large space currently occupied by silence. I know this silence. Parenting two sons has taught me that I cannot fill it; they may not fill it. "Am I missing something?" is a question I still ask myself all the time.

He is not talking much today. His hand holds a pen like the one that journaled his story that he left for a parent to find. His parents knew the diary told of his dejection and of his questioning whether his life had value. As he grew up, had he taken those early experiences and written a cohesively self-deprecating story that was larger than was apparent in those few sad moments he shared in my clinic? Given his health challenges, his sadness didn't seem to me to be unusual and actually seemed typical for his age and sensitivities. What story does he now carry into this protracted moment of his as a banner of perceived failure to fit in, to be connected, both in his own skin and in his 15-year-old peer group?

Sitting with him, I keep returning to his days as a little boy. Our tie should be that he sees the tremendous value I see in him, should it not? How do we help Eric rewrite his story as we see it, the main character Eric being strong, smart, worthy? As his doctor, along with his parents, I sought to have an imprint on his narrative, supporting and nurturing a positive story while he grew; yet we all know it is his to craft.

I appreciate that he did open up just that little bit today, telling me he is "OK" and he won't hurt himself. I have to respect his right to tell his story his way. And in letting his story be his, I am able to stand by him and be there if he needs me, not unlike my attempts to do this dance with my own sons. I may have incomplete information, but I am not going anywhere.

There is always so much I don't know about another. When I meet someone new or am working with a patient, I try to figure things out quickly. I ask questions and probe areas that I think will help me care more effectively for that person. I try to understand, to stand in someone's shoes for a few moments, but what do I really know? My knowledge is limited by time, by the other person's capacity to tell me, and also by feelings and preconceived notions I bring to the encounter. Even with my sons, I can only know what they will let me know and what I can understand. Knowing Eric reminds me there is so much I do not know. If I can shift my lens just a few degrees, I might see entirely different parts of a person's story. Strength can begin to look like a challenge, or in the midst of chaos there might actually be underlying and defining order.

Believing I know more than I actually know limits my opportunity to know more. With curiosity and open eyes maybe I will experience more shading, alternative interpretations, more than was seen and heard initially. If I hold a prior story as true, it requires humility to recognize that I did not get it all the first, second, or tenth time. Relationships with our patients are full of surprises, and when we find something out that we didn't know, or when what we thought we knew is turned upside down, we get a reminder that is useful throughout our lives.

The following stories speak of the authors' limited knowledge of another, where important information was not readily apparent, or where what was initially perceived might be part of a narrative that veiled a more complex reality.

Hidden Truths

Melanie Berg

In her broken English, she told me she was worried about her itchy legs. We call that her "chief complaint." There might have been a rash, I don't remember, probably because if there was a rash, you could hardly see it without good lighting and a magnifying glass. I spent fifteen minutes talking about skin hydration—about hot versus less hot showers, scented versus unscented lotion, abrasive drying versus pat-dry drying. Then she asked if she had given her son this rash. She said the rash on her son's face was severe, unresponsive to his doctor's treatments, and surely humiliating for an adolescent.

Aha! So this plump immigrant woman had come to see me for her nonexistent rash because she feels guilty about her son's more conspicuous facial lesions, which I had not seen. I reassured her that she did not bring this supposed teenage abomination of a facial rash upon her son. She seemed relieved to hear that. "Good." I told myself, "another successful visit, another happy client to add to my short list of same in the first year of residency." I gave my patient a sheet of instructions and nearly had my hand out to shake hers goodbye when she asked me: "Is there medication that can help with depression?"

Dismayed that I had failed to elicit the real reason for this visit before the last minute, I asked, "Why? Do you feel depressed?" Depending on the answer, I would likely have followed up with "We should make an appointment soon to talk more about this." We did not get there, as the narrative unfolded:

It was holiday season, and because her family was not Christian they didn't celebrate Christmas. But her teenage son and daughter were asking for Christmas presents. In a store she had seen some fancy and inexpensive bangles that she thought her daughter would enjoy. Having no money to purchase gifts, and believing no one would notice, she put them in her purse. She was caught and was expected to appear in court later in January.

"I've never stolen anything or even broken the law," she cried. "I feel such shame and I can't tell anyone in my family. They cannot find out." She finally revealed that she tried twice, between the time of the arrest and her visit with me, to jump in front of a moving car to kill herself. I was the first person she had told. Tears streaming down her face, her voice shook as she explained that there would be a letter coming to her house in the mail about her court appearance. She was certain that her family would find out, and was uncertain what her punishment would be. She was absolutely terrified of living in shame among her family. To her, this risk far outweighed any benefit of living at all.

As I listened to her and contemplated how I might help her, I came to the overwhelming realization that I didn't know what my patient had been experiencing, even as I tried to treat her. Forgetting the limits of my knowledge leads to erroneous conclusions all the time. On any given occasion, I have no idea what is going on in my patients' or anyone's lives. No idea.

Thank You David

Sherilyn Smith

Overbooked. 11:00 appointment, 30 minutes should be enough time for a hospital follow-up on a patient with osteomyelitis (infection in the bone). But his chart was huge (volume 3 of 4) and the discharge summary was missing. Oh good, my Infectious Disease Fellow (a doctor getting advanced special training in pediatric infectious diseases) knows the patient and can go see him quickly.

The Fellow returned swiftly and said David was taking his meds but the parents have some questions. She rolled her eyes. "Would it be O.K. if I go to see the next patient while you see him?" I agreed and went to meet David.

He was screaming and writhing in his wheelchair as I walked in the door. The noise was overwhelming. I smiled and moved to shake his father's hand. "David, stop it!" his father looked at David and tried to get him to stop. David didn't stop it. I moved toward him and he screamed louder, crying, rocking, and shaking his head. How did I miss that he had autism when I read his chart?

His father shook his head and said, "He always does this. Doctor, I was wondering what you thought about these papers about the genetic basis of macrocytosis? Have you read these papers?" as he handed me the reprints.

"No, I haven't read them."

"I was wondering if you think this might explain his macrocytosis"?

(Had I missed something? Macrocytosis?)

David had now taken off his clothes, was pulling at his ears, and was screaming, crying and rocking. Again Dad tried to redirect him and get him to stop. I wanted to cover my ears. I wondered, why me? Sigh. Redirect, take control, fail. Sigh. Try again.

"Is he taking his meds?"

"Yes, but only with Dr. Pepper and cheese crackers. That is all he will eat. Would you consider putting him on fluconazole? His cultures are negative, and I think that is a reasonable choice."

(What? Why was he saying this? There wasn't any fungus in the cultures.)

"Excuse me," I interrupted, "can you please tell me about your background? You seem to know more than most parents about science and medicine."

"Oh, well I'm a retired physician. I stay at home to take care of David and have time to do a lot of reading."

Sigh, wait, slow down, this is going to take a while, let go, listen. I had missed something.

This was all in the first five minutes of getting to know David and his family. The relationship lasted more than two years; it was not just a simple case of osteomyelitis. After several clinic visits with them, each visit unfolding at the same chaotic, barely manageable pace, I realized that I could never understand what it was like to be a parent for David. I couldn't understand what it meant to watch him eat, revel in his small successes, have dreams for him, and wish he were back to his old self, running around, communicative and happy, sure still naked except for his rubber boots. To a parent or a family, a child's illness is a deep, murky place full of emotions, experiences and wishes I could not understand, no matter how hard, how much, how often I tried. I would never get it.

So I stopped trying to understand the whys and the hows, and accepted that their experience was theirs, unique and important. This was liberating. I could care about them and care for them without needing to be them. By shedding light on their fears, rather than thinking I knew what their fears were, maybe I could help them face them. How humbling. There are things that are unknowable about other people.

So, now, with my patients and their parents, I try to see how their experience with illness shapes their questions and interactions with me. I let them show me what they can of their experience. If they don't share, I know it's still lurking there, affecting them, changing them and their family. Even when they do share, I know I can't fully understand the experience, but I acknowledge that it is there.

I won't ever fully understand why people act the way they act—racing up behind me and tailgating (Bad day? Argument? Talking to their kids?) or giving me a smile when I walk by (Habit? Recalling a memory? Anticipating the future?). Thinking we understand what drives people's actions so often just leads to misunderstandings and impatience.

Tolerance is a difficult thing to teach. Since I can never fully understand another's experience, I now choose to be more open and less reactive, appreciating that it's likely that I am missing something, just like the first time I met David. Sometimes gifts such as this understanding come from unexpected places. Thank you, David.

Postscript

David died at 19 years of age from complications of his complex medical problems. In speaking with his mom to obtain permission for the story, I learned much more about David than a single story can convey. This story, which is Dr. Smith's story of first meeting him, gives her perceptions of entering the room and encountering this child and his father. As his mother pointed out, it had to be overwhelming. She also noted that David was stressed and hurting and this was him at a low point, and not the full picture of who he was. Sometimes families who do not have disabled children don't remember that these individuals are so much more than what is seen in those "worst" moments. She talked about how Dr. Smith got to know David and his family and that several times she went to bat to advocate for surgery and treatment David urgently needed. She reminded me to not draw conclusions about David from the encounter shared here. He was a boy and then teen who did make connections, demonstrate caring, and in turn had friends and those who cared for him. He clearly touched many lives. As he approached death, former teachers and caregivers came from many miles to say good bye. Years after his death, former classmates still talk about their friend David. Sharon Dobie (ed)

What Was She "Seizing?"

Sharon Dobie

What changed for her? When Ms. R. comes to clinic now, she is mostly calm, always articulate, and only occasionally a bit worried about her symptoms or her kids. Fifteen years ago, this was not the case. Back then, she came to clinic worried and anxious. The biggest concerns were episodes that seemed like seizures. Periodically she would have one – at home, in clinic, anywhere – sometimes for unclear reason, sometimes when stress hit. She had been diagnosed with a seizure disorder, but about the time I met her, the neurologists were certain she was not having seizures and stopped her medication.

Ms. R. agreed to some counseling to help her figure out how to stop these spells. She sat down with her husband in the little counseling room of our clinic. The counselor began to ask questions. By about the third one, Ms. R's eyes rolled back into her head, and she appeared to lose consciousness but with no movement of her arms or legs. I was called to the room. Speaking softly to her, I found she was responsive, knew where she was, and could answer questions appropriately. Her husband said this is exactly what happened at home.

Was this her brain's unconscious way of literally leaving the scene when the topic was threatening or frightening? Was it a way to communicate her pain in a household where she felt the weight of responsibility was disproportionately on her shoulders? We all wondered what was happening and wanted the spells to stop. As counseling continued, she and her husband explored their relationship. Ms. R. and her husband had both operated within fairly structured cultural roles, yet neither expressed feeling bound by them.

Slowly, something in her changed. The passage of time, finding her voice, exploring work options, seeing her husband helping with household chores and parenting their daughters—who knows what? Somehow her perspective shifted, and the swooning episodes disappeared, taking with them much of the anxious worrying about everything. We never found out exactly what happened. It looked from the outside like she simply matured.

I recently asked her, but she still did not know or could not express, how she had taken a different hold on her life. Seizing, but now in a healthy way? Good reminder to me in that metaphor. Sometimes we just don't know. She seems comfortable with that. I am practicing.

Losing Part of Her
Sharon Dobie

She was in her mid-forties at that time, and neither of us expected complications from the forthcoming surgery. The way she had taken care of the arrangements did not surprise me: a note pad with checklist and organized questions. But I wondered what she was feeling, and asked her during one visit.

"It needs to be done, and I will be relieved to have it over and behind me.

Honestly, I have my kids, and my use of this uterus is over."

It was what I expected to hear: pragmatic, rational, and very like how I had seen her approach other issues and illnesses in the five years I had been her doctor. She had big fibroids in her uterus and was having heavy, annoying, and anemia-causing menstrual bleeding. After trying and failing to wrestle her bleeding into regularity with hormone pills and then with endometrial ablation (where a laser is used to surgically remove the lining of the uterus), she had decided to have a hysterectomy.

Her six-week leave from work was arranged and approved. She and her husband had gotten groceries and signed up friends to help in the initial post-operative days. Their young-adult children also planned to help. We all expected a routine surgery and rapid recovery without complications.

Several days after an uneventful operation she went home, and her physical recovery proceeded quickly. So when I saw that she was on my schedule about a month after surgery, I was surprised. Typically, she would have returned to see the surgeons after six weeks. Beside her name was a question: "depression?"

She looked well when I opened the door—neither gaunt nor swollen, dressed in comfortable jeans and a sweater, good color in her cheeks, make-up on, nails polished. Depression?

"Hi," I opened. "How are you? What's up?"

"I'm fine." She answered, though with a noticeable tremor in her voice. "But no one told me I would miss my uterus."

I asked her to tell me more, and her thoughts and feelings tumbled out.

"A good friend of mine is a really emotional person, and I figured if she had something like a mastectomy or hysterectomy or lost a foot or something, well, she would come all unglued. But not me. I knew I wanted the surgery, knew it would solve my problem. So why do I feel like I lost an old friend? Why am I so angry that no one told me I would feel like I had an amputation, like I am no longer whole? This can't be happening to me. I feel so guilty lying around all day, crying because part of me is gone. But I cannot seem to control it."

We had both been blindsided. For me it was a case of having thought I knew her and that her pragmatism would carry her easily through the experience. We had never spent time talking about her responses to other events that had happened in her life, events that might have uncovered some hints that she might feel loss after her hysterectomy and that it would require her to understand that sense of loss and learn to accept it. We had never explored the "what-ifs" of even the possibility of experiencing loss. Even if we had, would it have made a difference?

I thought I knew her. She thought she knew herself. In this case not knowing hindered her emotional preparation for her surgery. Over time she did come to accept both the loss and the unexpected, unsettling fact that she experienced it as a loss. Our relationship continues to remind me how little I really know about others or what is truly going on for them.

Chapter 10

My Patient as a Mirror

How She Handles ... No, How I Handle Frustration

Sharon Dobie

I hear her voice out at the front desk, raised. Our reception area is open at the back, providing a vista for those checking in at the front desk into the area where medical assistants weigh patients, where nurses meet with patients or talk with them on the phone, where doctors sit and work on charting. She is facing me, and one of our reception staff is listening to her with her back to me. When I hear my patient's voice, she is already fifteen minutes late for her fifteen-minute appointment with me. I have glanced up, unfortunately, and our eyes meet. She starts yelling to me, in the middle of clinic, gesticulating for me to come to the front. I shake my head no, pointing at what I am doing, as an act of either self-preservation or cowardice. A few seconds later the phone by my side rings. "Will you see T., or should she reschedule?" Our clinic policy is to reschedule a patient who is more than halfway through their allotted time when they arrive. We generally accommodate a wide variety of excuses, traffic being the most common one. I could still hear her agitated angry voice lecturing our staff out front. She was not letting up.

"Yeah. I'll see her."

T. is close to me in age. She's a tall, lean woman, well dressed whenever I see her. She has a master's degree, works in sales with a lot of public contact, and is quite successful in her career. For me she's a paradox. She usually arrives late (does she do that at business meetings?), and instead of apologizing she scowls and tells our front-desk staff she resents having to show her ID every time. Then, when our medical assistant asks to check her blood pressure, her first words often are, "No, I won't do that. Why do you always ask me?" Now, I have many patients who will not get on the scale, and neither will I, so I understand that one. Not having blood pressure taken is harder for me to understand. Weight is visible; blood pressure is not. While T. usually tells me why she has come, she often won't accept my recommendations, leaving me frequently uncertain of why she wanted to see me at all.

I like that she asks for the evidence when I recommend something and I know she can make up her own mind. But the edge of distrust and anger in her questions pushes my buttons. In talking through her options, she invariably levies a criticism about our staff, saying something like, "Why are your staff so pushy about taking blood pressures and my being late, since you always keep me waiting? I don't see why I have to come in when you could take care of almost all my needs by email." No matter that there are many if not most issues where I like to actually talk with and see the patient!

In short, I am an irritating gnat in her life, or so I feel. Should I humbly apologize for occasionally running behind? Debate her point with all the defensiveness I can muster about how relatively prompt I am? Tackle the email question? (At this point maybe she should take my blood pressure.) We are doing more email communication with patients, but sometimes I need to examine the person, or maybe I need the face-to-face contact to review medication side effects or talk through a given therapy. Email does not let me see the person's eyes or emotions that might be helpful to our interaction.

Actually, her irritability and argumentativeness leave me even less open to meeting many of her needs by email. I need to see her, observe her affect, and hear her discussion in real time to be able to present my thoughts and recommendations, to understand how she is making her decisions about my recommendations, and to accept that I have done my part in our partnership. Her prickly negativity is a barrier to knowing her and supporting her, and we just do not work very well together. I am always on edge with her and I'm not alone with those feelings. A number of our clinic staff are a little afraid of her and feel demeaned by her. It takes me more time and care to reassure myself that I have done enough for her.

That she continues to return to our clinic says something, but I'm not sure what. Maybe she's getting some of her needs met. But which needs? Maybe other doctors and clinics irritate her even more. Is it some underlying anxiety about her health or a history of treatment by the health care system that leaves her particularly cantankerous? Maybe this is the way she is elsewhere and not just with us. Or maybe her relationships in other arenas are smooth, and it's just us who are not adequate in her eyes. But she comes back. I suspect I will never know the answers to these questions, because so far my attempts to ask have been met with criticisms of us and of our work. So now I work on how I can work with her. We have told her that polite behavior towards staff is requisite to getting care in our clinic, and that when she's late, we can address less of what is on her list.

When I look closely at my irritation with T., the traits that bother me resemble my own bothersome traits. Recently I was on the phone with an insurer and was not getting what I wanted from them. Frustrated, I saw myself from the outside. And next to me in my mind's eye, helping me to modulate, was this barometer showing levels of frustration. The upper levels were ones I did not want to reach, represented by T.'s contorted and angry face.

Sometimes our patients and our interactions with them offer a look in the mirror, a glimpse of who we really are, bringing to the surface events, feelings, or realizations and affording us greater self-understanding that otherwise would be elusive.

Reminder
Erin Richardson

Recently I visited with an elderly patient with severe anemia; we were admitting her to the hospital. She had advanced dementia and could no longer talk. Speaking to the patient's husband about how much medical intervention he would want to pursue for his wife, I reviewed a fairly standard list of reasons why we would recommend, because of her dementia, not being very aggressive in her care. He became silent after I finished talking and it caught me off guard. I realized I had been speaking to him almost mechanically. He looked up with tears in his eyes and asked, "What should I do? Really, what can I do?"

It almost took my breath away. A flood of emotions and thoughts raced through my mind. I was ashamed for acting so much like a machine, like the doctor I never wanted to be, the doctor who rattles off lists and reasons based on objective evidence but detached from the person needing care. That emotion gave way to an unexpected realization of the beauty of this couple's intimate lifelong relationship. Those were the feelings I took home with me. I thought of my husband and me, hoping that some day we would have that relationship, and wanting to give him the courage to let me go when it was time. I reflected on my parents, struggling to imagine how one of them would survive without the other and also feeling that time with family is so dear. I have already started to plan my next years differently—with multiple vacations to visit my family.

Swastika

Stephanie Cooper

Let his swastika be a lesson to me—the enormous faded blue swastika tattooed on his chest.

They had asked me, queer Jew doctor girl, to sew up his face. He had a complex, stellate laceration deep enough that I could run my finger across his filleted forehead and touch the white grit of his frontal bone. He was rather unconscious, responding to sternal rubs and "hey-hey-Dave-are-you-still-with-me?" Still, I numbed him up plentifully, compassionately, but also aware of my power, knowing that as he slumbered in morphine-laden sleep, I could ruin his face with my suture, sculpt a jagged or too-tight skin fold, make the eyes of future others fix upon an ugly scar. But I didn't want that, even if he was a skinhead, even if he might hate everything about me. I sewed him up with pride in my work as always, the edges neatly approximating, the fractured puzzle pieces annealed into a smooth plane. The doc before me had told me his CT scans and films all "looked fine." So without checking the X-rays myself, I sent him home.

Maybe if he had been a nice, normal citizen I would have checked his X-rays, would have at least looked through the films and CT scans myself, not waiting for the radiologist's report. Perhaps if he looked like me, or was gay, or smiled benevolently, or had even one quality that endeared him to me despite the swastika. Instead, I labeled him as a skinhead methadone addict on disability, who had crashed his car due to negligence and overmedication, someone who was frittering away hard-earned money taken from people like me. I didn't like him, based on his tattoo. His ugly, garishly large, Jew-hatin' swastika. As I was sewing up his face, I thought about telling him I am Jewish, and gay.

I sent him home, imagining his wife and him driving in silence or perhaps to religious AM radio back to Hayden Lake or the local Aryan compound, having given him half his methadone dose out of pity. About an hour after he left, out of curiosity I looked at the X-rays and had to read the report over several times: "small hairline lucency of the right acetabulum which could be consistent with fracture." Crap! I had sent the guy home with a fractured hip! Fixated on getting swastika-man out of my ER and away from me, I hadn't even watched him walk or stand!

Ashamed, I had to call him back to the ER. Several hours later he arrived holding the green piece of paper commanding him to see me. Luckily for everyone, the additional X-rays of his hip looked normal, and I made sure that he could walk painlessly and had full range of his legs before I sent him home. Now that he was dressed and bandaged, nobody could see the glaring tattoo that had so offended me.

I had judged him to be a bigoted Neo-Nazi skinhead, but of the two of us, I clearly held the more damaging prejudice. He was the patient, and I was the doctor, and his beliefs and politics and tattoos shouldn't influence how I treated him. All that should matter is that he needed help and that I could and would help him. Instead, blinded by his fading swastika, I became the narrow-minded bigot. I had kept my judgment bottled up inside. He at least wore his symbol of hatred where it could be seen.

Many Ways to Love
Anonymous

"You're here to have an abortion today. Are you sure this is what you want to do?"

The woman's eyes were red when I'd walked into the room so I sat down, put my hand on her shoulder, and asked her the question as gently as I could. She nodded, lips quivering. I waited a few moments. She added "It's just that I have always wanted to be a mother, and ..." she started sobbing and put her hand on her belly.

"I already feel attached."

She was nine weeks pregnant. She was twenty years old.

I said nothing, but my first thought was not about her, it was about me. I had a two-year old at home and had not felt attached to him when I was nine weeks pregnant, or when I was twenty-nine or thirty-nine weeks. I'd had friends who fell in love with their children as soon as the home pregnancy test turned positive. Other friends developed the radiant smile when their babies started kicking. But I hadn't felt anything like that during pregnancy or even when my son was first born. Here was a woman with an unplanned, unwanted pregnancy and she felt attached already. Had there been something wrong with me? Was there still?

I'd had a lot of ambivalence about having children and had procrastinated as long as I could. During my pregnancy I avoided thinking about my inevitable motherhood. I was worried I wouldn't be up to the task. Children made me feel awkward. I tried to connect with them: I ooohed and ahhed over babies, read books and kicked soccer balls with my young relatives, but it was exhausting and always felt forced. Adult company was so much easier.

Right when I first became pregnant, I started doing abortions again, moonlighting occasionally in a small town. Would it be strange serving women who did not want to be pregnant as my own belly grew? The patients though were eager to talk about it, especially the women who already had children. They gave me advice on how to cope with labor pains and lack of sleep, on how to raise young toddlers and sassy teenagers. Half the women who have abortions are already mothers, and my patients with children talked about their kids easily and comfortably and shared their sad stories too—struggles with money, men, and work. But they were always proud when telling me about their kids. I heard about their infants that were crawling, toddlers' first words, school-aged sports stars, and high-schoolers getting ready for college. I wondered if I would ever want to talk about my child like that. What would he do that would cause me to rave about him to perfect strangers?

When I had my son, I held him and was overwhelmed by his neediness and fragility. I felt the huge responsibility of keeping him safe, but I did not fall in love. I did the things I was supposed to do: I nursed him, I rocked him, I talked to him even when it felt ridiculous and I had nothing to say. I kept asking my husband if he loved the baby, inexplicably concerned that he would bond first. I worried about my son, checking often at night to make sure he was still breathing. I wondered if that was all there was—whether the anxiety was the only facet of love that I would experience.

Learning to love my son happened gradually and continually. And it happened much faster once he could express his feelings for me. At six months, his face would light up with his toothless smile when I walked into a room. He would flap his arms and squeal to indicate that he wanted me to pick him up, and he would nuzzle his face into my shoulder when he was tired. At thirteen months, when he started walking, I was so proud that I had to choke down my instincts to immediately tell everyone in the neighborhood. And when he started talking I laughed every day about something hilarious that he said. And while I still feel awkward around other children, I joyfully sing and dance for him without a speck of self-consciousness. I hug him and cover him with kisses even when he wants to wiggle away. Even just writing these words about him fills me with a happy glow.

And that's just it: that glow. That is why women having abortions, who are vulnerable and anxious, talk about their children. There is a range of emotion in an abortion clinic that encompasses guilt, disappointment, determination, and relief. (As one young woman explained it to me, with tears running over her freckles, "no little girl ever dreams that she's going to grow up and have an abortion".) But the women who are already mothers are usually more at peace. Before, I'd attributed it to a combination of things – they aren't worried that they're missing their only chance to be a parent; they have the certainty that they are helping their children; they have more life experience and perspective. But now I understand how, when you love a child, just picturing their face, talking about them, fills you with a distracting warm feeling. It is easy to think about your child and it makes pain, shame, and fear fade into the background.

The twenty-year old woman who felt attached to her nine-week old fetus went ahead with the abortion. She was certain it wasn't the right time to have a child; she had no support. But most likely she will experience that attachment again in the future, and I've learned that it will grow and change into feelings that she can't possibly imagine now.

Parents fall in love with their children at different times, in different ways, and this love changes constantly as both kids and parents grow. My patients showed me my future; I just couldn't comprehend it at the time.

Insatiable
Anonymous

After so many years in clinic, I recognize most names on my schedule. Usually I feel delight, less often neutrality, rarely a mild dismay on seeing one name or another. But these emotions are in marked contrast to the intense sinking feeling when I see MT's name. The sinking is actually the sensation that my stomach is dropping, like it does on the steep rapid descent on a roller coaster, but without the associated thrill. Instead, there is the associated dry mouth and involuntary clenching of my fists. It is a toxic mix of "I don't want to go in there" and hating myself for feeling that way.

I first encountered him as the person pushing the wheelchair of another one of my patients into the exam room. The woman in the wheelchair on that day and many other days was in her late forties. He would bring her to the exam room, leaning into the handlebars of the doublewide wheelchair, his face red and sweaty, breathless, the effort taking all his strength. He was in his early fifties and also clearly not in the best of health. She had a non-stop frowning monologue, continuously criticizing his driving skills: "Can't you see?" "What are you trying to do, break my leg on the door frame?"

Maneuvering that large wheelchair through the too-small doorway he would simply respond, "I'm sorry, sweetie, I'm doing the best I can." He would turn his puppy dog eyes on me. "You'll have to forgive her, doctor. She gets so frustrated and she just can't help it."

He stayed in the room during her visits with me, adjusting her chair, her oxygen tank, or whatever other task she assigned him. She complained about everything in her life but had an endlessly expanding list of reasons why she could not change her behavior or follow recommendations that might improve things. He would frequently look at me beseechingly, asking me to help her stop killing herself. Sometimes he sounded like the parent of a rebellious adolescent.

"Doctor, tell her she needs to lose weight, needs to elevate her legs. Can't you do something to make her do it?" Then he would plead with her, "Honey see, the doctor wants you to stop eating so much and to take your medicine. Please do it for me."

It was endless variations on the same theme. At times he sounded like a tattletale trying to please me with inside information. "She is killing herself," he would report as he described days of her not moving out of her wheelchair, not wearing her breathing machine at night, and continuing to eat the amount of food required to maintain her 400-plus pounds. I never had the courage to ask why he didn't stop bringing the food to her—I think he was afraid of displeasing her, and I was afraid to hear that, or hear her response.

One morning he found her dead in her chair. I was as shocked as he was. Although we both knew she was very ill, neither of us expected her death to come so quickly. After a few phone conversations with attempting to comfort him and offering my condolences, he himself became my patient. His name appeared on my schedule rather frequently, almost monthly. With each subsequent appearance, upon seeing his name, the sinking feeling in my stomach became more pronounced. All of our visits began with his sadness over her death and his statements that she did it to herself despite his best efforts. He thanked me repeatedly for the supportive phone calls and frequently said he didn't know what he would do without me. With each repetition of this litany, I squirmed more and found myself having to exert incredible self-control not to just blurt out "Stop it."

MT never failed to tell me that the waiting room was full of patients praising me, that he had never been to such a great doctor, and that the only reason he commuted such a great distance to this clinic was to see me. "Doctor, you know, you're the greatest. No one else listens like you do. All of us in the waiting room agree that you are worth the wait." I wondered what he wanted from me. No one could be troweling it on this thick without an agenda, but he never asked for drugs, disability forms, or any of the things I thought he might be angling for.

During each visit, after the praise litany we would move on to his medical issues, all of which were to some extent affected by his obesity. He would describe coming home from the grocery store to consume extraordinary quantities of high-calorie food, and feeling incapable of controlling this hunger.

Interspersed with questions about his blood pressure and weight, he always had questions about his sexual function. He would tell me about his new relationship in a little more detail than I wanted to know, but not necessarily inappropriate for one's doctor.

I would frequently turn away, finding eye contact with him very uncomfortable. I wondered whether his eyes really were wandering over me in a way which felt invasive or whether I was just imagining things. One day he told me a button on my blouse (which was covered by my white coat) was undone. Provocative male patients in the past usually didn't make me uncomfortable, but with MT I always felt uncomfortable and exposed.

Teaching residents and students how to interact with patients, I encourage them to mentally erase their biases prior to entering the patient's room; I ask them to identify pre-existing judgments within themselves and try to set them aside in order to operate from a nonjudgmental standpoint. But here I was, filled with judgment and a 50-50 mix of guilt and revulsion each time MT's name was on my schedule. Why was I so uncomfortable with him?

Reflecting now, I realize the revulsion was at least partly directed at myself for being such a hypocrite, for failing to be able to take the advice that I dole out readily to my children and trainees. I was sure that he could sense my discomfort with him and surer that he knew deep down that I was a very small person incapable of treating him without judgment.

With a change in insurance plans, he moved on to another doctor. Now years later, I further understand my discomfort. He embodies and showed me many characteristics that I possess but wish I did not have. We all have shadow sides, parts of ourselves which are not noble, self-sacrificing, or worthy, but my self-image as a person and a doctor had no room for my shadow side.

The elements of my own shadow were clearly manifested and exaggerated in MT. His obsequiousness, need to please others, and his unrestrained hunger are all aspects of myself that I reject. Exhibiting compassion and acceptance for these characteristics in another human being would perhaps force me to acknowledge and accept them in myself, so I had to keep MT distant and separate. If I opened myself to seeing him from a nonjudgmental, compassionate standpoint, I would have to see my shadow and myself in the same way.

Self-Care
Anonymous

Jackie and I were good friends. We often studied together and met before every exam for a final cram session. At such a big medical school, we were lucky to get assigned to a prime rotation together. The teaching doctors there had great reputations, and a good recommendation from one of them would serve us well. We were staying with John, Jackie's good friend from high school. He was a medical student at another school and rotating at the same hospital. The three of us got along famously and often met for post-call breakfast.

One evening when we were on call, Jackie called John at home to plan our post-call breakfast. Suddenly she looked alarmed, and was obviously trying to sound calm. After a minute or two she wrote on a piece of paper "John cut his wrists." He wasn't bleeding much, by his report. Jackie was trying to determine how stable he was, and if someone could bring him in. But John was hesitant. He knew many of the doctors at the hospital and didn't want to be identified. No one else was available to pick him up.

For a moment I hesitated to interrupt my work, thinking about how important this rotation was. If I could just squeeze a strong recommendation out of it, I might have my pick of residencies and be on my way to medical stardom. But the mission of being a physician was worthless and false if I chose training over helping a friend who was hurt.

Jackie went to get John while I stayed on the phone talking with him until she got there. I said some of the wrong things to John, and we laughed and he coached me in my counseling. He was well aware of the dynamics going on. He and I discussed what he would and would not accept in the way of care. His cuts would have to be sewn up, but he didn't want any of that evening's team doing it, because he knew them.

Our hospital had the only emergency department open at these hours. Jackie brought him in though because we did not see many options. Somehow it became clear that I was going to sew him up. And I did. I think I used the wrong kind of suture and I didn't really know how to do the stitches. But I did it.

John was clear that he was not going to try to hurt himself again, and over the next few days he saw his psychiatrist and got the care he needed. I learned later that he had been in the midst of adjusting his psychiatric prescriptions. I hadn't known he had a psychiatric history. He was a high-functioning guy with a difficult past, including family abuse, family substance abuse, and a brother who had committed suicide. The cutting incident had occurred on the anniversary of his brother's death.

That night with John put things in perspective for me. Like my fellow students, in training and after, I strove to be superhuman. We worked insane hours on unwise minimums of sleep; we lost weight and we gained weight. We trained ourselves to focus and think faster, harder. We denied our emotions and our physical needs, not to mention social and psychological needs. Sometimes in the process we forgot our humanity, elevating our goals above it. But when we do that, as I knew even then – when we stop being human – we lose our ability to hear and treat our human patients.

Like me, John was a physician in training, and smart. He picked up ideas quickly and studied hard. He had a wealth of information and his conversations were provocative, covering a wide range of topics. He excelled in training and is a well-respected physician now. Our experience that night made it so clear that he was human—which had to mean, since he was a mirror of me and I of him, that I was human and vulnerable as well.

I was and still am at risk of pushing so hard, fast, and independently that I put myself physically and mentally at risk. The lesson was there that night with John, but I didn't learn it. I still held myself to a superhuman standard. During the first four months of residency, I became so thin that I was on Ensure for a year and a half to maintain my weight. And still I did not learn. I once called a friend on my cell phone to stay awake on my drive home after a sleepless 36-hour shift. I got home safely but the next week I could not remember anything we had talked about.

When does my work become my life? How do I choose and control that? Am I a friend, a wife, a mother before, after, or while I am a doctor?

When my girlfriend was in the hospital with stroke symptoms, visiting her in the hospital meant foregoing a mother-daughter afternoon. When my son stuck a bead in his ear, I had to cancel my last seven patients and pick him up from school. When my patient needs to go to the Emergency Department right now, should I stay in clinic and arrange the transfer, even if I miss the Kindergarten party? The time to organize home care for a patient with daily seizures can come out of my free time, or it can wait until next week. Maybe I need to increase my work hours, yet if do, will I really be a better doctor or will I just be a less-present Mom? If I find a nanny so I can work more, am I setting a good example of balance for my kids or just weaseling out of the harder job of parenting and house management?

Like John, like my patients, I am human. Juggling the dynamic demands and responsibilities of life is challenging and elusive. Remembering that there are choices – remembering John – helps.

Permission

Anonymous

I looked at the ER board again, hoping for a straightforward medical case. Again, I saw "6 y/o - behavior problem," with no physician signed up and a wait time of 0:42. Each of us had avoided seeing her, and no wonder: who would want to jump into a six-year-old's behavioral issue in the emergency room? Sounded ominous to me. But that had been a long wait, so I decided I would try.

On the hospital gurney was a petite little girl in a princess dress, asleep, surrounded by crayons – the 6-year-old "behavior problem." Next to her was a woman, presumably her mother, with puffy red eyes. This young mother had five children, including a set of infant twins. She was trying desperately to keep house, go to college, and care for her children while her husband was busy at work. Her story about the girl on the gurney tumbled out, a jealous child who had never seemed to adjust to the birth of her twin brothers. She was angry, throwing frequent tantrums (and objects) and biting her siblings. Her mother felt trapped and torn.

"I don't know what to do. If I lock her in her room, she just carries on more. The only thing that quiets her is a big dose of Benadryl, and I know that is not good for her either. But I have to protect the babies, and keep her from hurting herself."

With her hand on my arm, as I walked out to speak with my attending, she looked at me and said, "Please ..." She was essentially saying, "This is bigger than me, and I can't do it alone." This mother had come to our emergency room to pass on a burden she was no longer able to carry herself. She wasn't asking for drugs, for hospitalization, for tests. Instead, she was asking to be heard and understood, to find a way to share the responsibility of keeping the family whole and well. I believed she was also asking for permission to take back a small part of her life, just for herself.

That shift coincided with the week my partner of eight years was moving out, at my request. I had spent years focusing on how to keep him from destroying his life financially, at considerable cost to my own happiness. By asking him (finally) to leave, I too was taking a step to reclaim my life. I felt a wave of connection between myself and the young mother, and a mutual sense of giving permission to be scared, overwhelmed, and to try to grow and heal.

Testicles and Other Fears
Irf Asif

On the chart was the chief complaint of "testicular pain." I had two simultaneous thoughts. One took me back to my days in medical school. I had a friend in medical school named Bob, a great guy. Bob just liked to have fun and wasn't worried about his grades or how he did in class, which sometimes was a good thing, and sometimes not. But, whenever I needed to gain a different perspective about school or life, or when it needed to be reiterated to me that there was more to life than school and stress, I went to him to let loose.

Late in medical school, Bob announced that he had found a bump on his testicle and was informed that he had testicular cancer. He went through chemotherapy and radiation, even had his sperm frozen. A few months later, he and his wife became pregnant and eventually had a baby girl. Unfortunately, she was born with a cardiac condition and had several corrective procedures early in her newborn life. That this family overall is coping well, I am sure is in part because of Bob's good-hearted, optimistic nature, and laid-back personality.

The second thought, as I looked at that chart, was about myself. A few weeks before, I felt a nodule around my testicle that was quite painful. I wasn't sure what it was or even how long it had been there. I was almost certain that it wasn't cancer, but I immediately thought back about Bob and his experience. I looked in anatomy books and "Up to Date" for information, and told myself it would go away. I didn't remember any trauma that would have caused the nodule to form. It wasn't related to sexual experiences—my girlfriend was 3,000 miles away and we hadn't seen each other in several months. So where did it come from?

During that time a patient had come in with a marble-sized swelling in his testicle that turned out to be benign, so mine was probably benign as well, right? The pain lasted nine days, and then it was gone. Relieved, I decided that it was somehow related to trauma on the soccer field or in friendly basketball game, and let it go.

It was three days after the nodule went away when I saw that chart on my exam room door saying the patient had testicular pain. An employee at the university where I worked, he felt almost like family. He said a lump had been there for two weeks and now it was painful. On exam, the testicle felt enlarged, and irregular in consistency, like a kiwi. I told the patient I thought it was cancer, based on my exam, although to be honest, I had never felt one before in this location. Four days later, he had an ultrasound report consistent with testicular cancer.

I thought about my experience a few weeks earlier. How anxious and nervous I had been when I had felt a nodule that luckily was not malignant. I tried to place myself in my patient's shoes to imagine how he felt, and those feelings multiplied exponentially, making me almost sick inside. I thought about Bob and what he had gone through during the difficulties and stresses of medical school. It was one of those soul-revealing moments where I realized that the tribulations in my life are merely drops, while Bob's and this patient's cancers felt more like an ocean-sized flood.

My patient came for an appointment to go over the ultrasound results, and I told him the news. He tried to stay positive. I could not believe how well he handled me telling him. It was almost as if he was taking care of me. Or was it denial? Later in the visit, he opened up more and I saw his anger at having the diagnosis. We talked, I listened. He talked, I listened. He left to schedule his appointment for surgery. I think about this man often.

"Testicular pain" or "ball pain" are chief complaints that young men often have. Most times they turn out to be nothing serious. True for me and not so for Bob and this patient. Well, now I had a different perspective on this symptom and on how we handle the worry and the diagnoses in various ways.

Bob is a happy-go-lucky person who always seemed to find a positive way to meet whatever challenges he faced. When something happens to me, though, I let it get to me. I can sulk. After anterior cruciate ligament surgery on my knee, I looked down at my knee and could not get the muscle to contract. Though I knew things could be much worse, it was still a tearful experience for me. But as a care provider, I try to stay positive with my patients. They can tell, and it helps them to be positive. Bob and this patient's efforts remind me that with my own trials, staying positive can help me eventually find a way to deal with challenges and move on.

Mothers
Sharon Dobie

That Sunday was like any weekend day on call as a second-year resident for our hospital's adult family medicine service. At 8 AM, the team would start walking together to see all the patients, discuss their progress, and make plans for the day. To be ready for these "rounds" at 8, I arrived by at least 7:15 to see all my patients. I checked with the nurses for any concerns, then asked each patient how he or she was feeling and what had happened the day before when I was not there. I listened to their hearts and lungs, examined their abdomens and any other parts of their bodies relevant to why they were in the hospital. Then I reviewed the nursing record of their blood pressures, pulses, temperatures, and respiration checks from the prior twenty-four hours, as well as any laboratory results. Our team visited each patient; one of us presented an oral summary and we would visit with and examine the patient together.

Once I got started with the work and visiting with the patients, I could usually get in the groove of being on call. The camaraderie of the team and the hospital staff, the almost rhythmic cadence of the day and night, the excitement of the unexpected, and the hope of tricking fate for a little sleep would carry me forward, oblivious to anything outside of the hospital walls and the immediacy of the beeps from my pager that punctuated every few minutes. I won't lie and say I loved the long hours and being on call on a weekend. But I could do it, and with good humor most of the time.

Not that day. I don't remember how I had spent Saturday, but Sunday should have felt like just another day on call, and it did not. I felt crabby. I did not want to be there. I could do the work, but I just could not get cheerful with myself or figure out why.

Standing at the counter by one patient's room, I was writing a lab order and feeling out of sorts, when looking at that room brought back a memory. About a year earlier, Remedios, a 39 year-old woman, was in that room dying of a rare cancer, a leiomyosarcoma of her uterus. Several years earlier, she had come to the United States as a licensed practical nurse from the Philippines, leaving her two young children with their grandparents. She saved her money and sent it home to support the family, planning to eventually send for her children. Her illness changed everything.

Remedios had a hysterectomy, removing her uterus, ovaries and fallopian tubes, but there was visible cancer left behind. She hoped she would become healthy enough to travel back to the Philippines to see her children, but her cancer had a different idea. It was aggressive, and, in the days before we had palliative and home hospice care, Remedios was in the hospital for pain management. She was dying. During the first week of her admission, our social worker and I spent hours talking with the State Department and the consulates, and asking airlines for compassionate assistance to bring her children to see her. Our efforts failed, and Remedios died alone.

Standing outside her room that Sunday, a year or so after her death, I had another memory. During Remedios' last hospitalization, another young woman had been getting ready to have her first baby. She was "my" first pregnant patient, for whom I had provided prenatal care throughout her pregnancy. She came with her husband to the hospital, in labor. Several times, while she labored, I ran downstairs to sit for a few minutes with Remedios, who was no longer conscious. I delivered this couple's first child while Remedios was dying a couple of floors below.

On the Sunday in question, a year later, I was standing with my memories and my crabby mood outside that room when a nurse friend of mine stopped by our ward. She took me aside and said, "Here's a hug. I know today must be a difficult day for you."

"Why?" I asked, not hiding my surprise. How did she know I was out of sorts that day? Her reply stopped me dead in my tracks.

"Because it's Mother's Day."

My mother had died only three months before, yet I had no conscious awareness that this day on call was Mother's Day. I thought about the two mothers in my care the year before and on my mind that day. Even though they did not know my story, I felt their lives and stories were connected with mine. Realizing it was Mother's Day, and registering its relevance for me that year, my mood shifted from irritable and unsettled to incredibly sad over real and imagined losses mirrored in the lives that touched mine. I was reminded that I was a person, whose life was unfolding during and within my life as a doctor and was much more than just my life in medicine.

Chapter 11

Self-Acceptance

Good Enough[5]
Sharon Dobie

His disheveled appearance and shuffling gait sharply contrasted with the purposeful walk of the bike-helmeted professional in pressed jeans from only six years earlier. It was a visual reminder of a process I could not seem to affect. I wanted him to get better. It did not matter who made him better. It could be his work, the efforts of his other doctors, the medicines, or some twist of fate as unexpected as whatever put him in this shadow state. It is maybe easiest to feel good about my work and who I am when my patient gets better, gets over the illness, is fixed, cured. In this case, I didn't need to be the effective one. I simply wanted him to be well. His not improving was linked to my dread when he was on my schedule. Doctors can be hard on themselves. I can be hard on myself.

When I first met him, he was in his early forties, a project manager in a growing technical field, up for a promotion. He rode his bike everywhere despite an old knee injury, saying, "Of course I ride. More people should ride for the sake of our environment, and my knee actually is better when I keep it moving." He was married with three children, sharing with me that he did half of the childcare, was a room parent at school, coached a soccer team, and loved helping his kids with their homework. In those early encounters his voice was confident and his mood seemed calm when he described a life that appeared engaged and thriving.

He came to me in search of more effective relief of pain from that old knee injury. Every few months we laboriously reviewed the materials

---

5   This story was first published in *The Healing Art of Writing*, J. Baranow, D. Watts, and B. Dolan (editors), UC Medical Humanities Press, 2010.

from prior evaluations. He carried a bulging file of X-Rays, MRIs, physical therapy reports, and notes from visits with orthopedic, pain, and neurology physicians. These records from the other doctors all agreed on a diagnosis of osteoarthritis. But there was also a deeper anxiety and compulsion, suggested by the frequency of his visits and his reluctance to accept that his prior evaluations and treatments had been both informative and exhaustive. Each time he came to see me, he would ask, "Might it be something else? Are we missing something that's worse or something that could be made better?" Although he said he lived with daily pain, he also said it didn't affect or limit his work or physical activity. Citing time and cost reasons, he declined the physical therapy, massage, and acupuncture I offered. He said he only wanted to know what was wrong and whether it was something worse.

"What do you think it is?" I would ask.

"I don't know. I just want the pain to go away. I want to know what is causing the pain."

We would again review all the tests that had been done and whether more testing was needed. During most visits I asked about his mood, and he insisted he was fine.

"You seem to worry. Are you kind of anxious?" I would ask.

"Pain gets you down, ya know. I don't like to not be able to move around without pain. And I worry that I have a bad disease. Sometimes I'm a little depressed." I suggested counseling and antidepressants; he declined them.

About two years into our relationship, he developed new symptoms of abdominal and chest pain. A treadmill test, some blood tests, and an ultrasound were reassuringly normal. Pain continued to be the main theme of our discussions. Most of the time it was his old knee pain. Sometimes it was the chest or abdominal pain or a new pain, but always pain, always physical pain. Often he rated it at 8 out of 10, with 10 representing severe pain.

He admitted to feeling sad and dejected more often when these new pains appeared. He denied most other symptoms associated with depression, including any thoughts of harming himself or someone else. Though he adamantly held to the belief that the pain was the problem, he agreed to work with a former counselor of his and to take an antidepressant medication. In a subsequent visit, he said he was feeling much better and that the counseling was helping him to feel calmer.

Then over the next few months, he appeared to unravel. He came to one appointment frowning and would not sit down. His speech was rapid and his blood pressure was elevated. As he paced around the tiny exam room, hands never quiet, he admitted to stopping his antidepressant and said that he and his wife had separated. His voice rose as he said that at work he had asked for a transfer to a different section in his office and that the response was to terminate him. "I'm going to file for unemployment and fight the termination," he said. "OK, so I have had my mind on other things and have not gotten all of my work done. I will look for other work." As his pacing increased, I felt my blood pressure rising. His rapid, loud, emphatic monologue continued for several minutes.

When I was able to interrupt, I asked him about his medications and why he had stopped them. I asked him if he had thoughts of hurting himself or others. I asked about his separation from his wife. "I can't talk about it. I have no interest in hurting myself. The problem is my pain. I won't discuss this any more. It is always the same pain. I will be fine if you will just take my pain away!" he kept insisting. At this visit, his pain was in his hip and groin. He said he could not afford physical therapy and massage, so I suggested some exercises for him and we discussed a regimen of daily medication. I stressed how concerned I was about his emotional state, recommending that he restart his antidepressant medication and have a consultation with a psychiatrist. He agreed to see his counselor the next day, to consult with a psychiatrist, and to reconsider medication.

I saw him several times soon after that. Despite his psychiatric care and medications, over the next few months he became a shadow person. To me it seemed the change was overnight. I could hardly see in him the person I had known; I would not have recognized him on the street. His clothes became wrinkled and his hair uncut. His posture was stooped. His voice became so quiet that he seemed to be disappearing into himself. All he would discuss was his pain. "I will be fine if you will make this pain go away. I am in terrible pain all the time." We reviewed all his prior tests and repeated some. I reinforced his work with psychiatry. He was back on an antidepressant and seeing his counselor, but he said he had no relief to his pain.

I shared my thoughts. "I can't tell you what part of your pain is from the arthritis and what part is because you are depressed. What I do know is that when someone is depressed, as you are now, that person will feel pain more intensely. It is real pain. The treatments are the exercises, staying active, taking the medications, and then really working hard with your counselor and psychiatrist to resolve your depression." We tried medications for the pain and he agreed to resume physical activity. At this point I was anxious for him, but still hopeful that his care team would bring him out of his depression and help his pain.

At an appointment a few weeks later, he became agitated, started pacing, and told me he had made a grave mistake and could not forgive himself. "I am ashamed of what I did and I deserve to feel guilty." He disclosed that his pain was worse when he was feeling guilty. "I betrayed my family and I cannot live with myself," he said and he would not tell me more. Our Mental Health Professionals offered him voluntary admission that day, which he declined. They did not think he was in imminent danger of self-harm. The next day he went to the emergency room, talked of ending his life, and was hospitalized.

After being discharged from the hospital, he moved with reluctance, became uncommunicative, and wore his depression with a frightening countenance. Some of it was the medication and some seemed to be the expression of his current emotional reality. He seemed three inches shorter. Each step he took was small and tentative, like a person with Parkinson's disease. His hands now trembled and could not be still. His face looked immobile, empty, and expressionless, like a face in a wax museum. It was as if he put on a costume for a theatrical role: "Now I *am* a depression. There is nothing else to me."

Over the next several years he was hospitalized a number of times. Usually a suicide note found by his son or a method or plan left for and found by his separated wife precipitated these hospitalizations; occasionally he just knew he needed to be in the hospital. His children kept going to school, but told their mom they worried all the time. His wife went to work and they all talked with a counselor. Yet who knows what the outside world really understood about this family? Only occasionally did it seem as if the medications and work with the psychiatric team were effective. In those periods, his pain was also better and he got back on his bike and was active. But after a brief interlude the symptoms would return, and he would again say his pain was worse, that he felt paralyzed, that he was thinking of ending his life. He would be readmitted for medication adjustment and counseling and then discharged after anywhere from days to weeks. He met with his mental health team every week or two and came to see me once or twice a month.

That is my attempt to tell his story as I saw it, the parts he let me see and hear, my rendition of his story. And there is more, of course. There is all I cannot know about him and his story. And then there is our relationship, because I was his doctor, which of course influences how I tell his story and the story of our doctor-patient relationship.

Early on, I felt like the second opinion doctor, reviewing the extensive work of others, helping him to understand – no, to accept – what the reports said, reassuring him, and encouraging him to stay active and take occasional over-the-counter medications. Our conversations felt amiable and collaborative to me, even with his many worried questions and the appointments that lasted longer than the allocated fifteen minutes. Yet I worried that I would not be able to help this man; his pain was not improving and he did not ascribe it to any emotional or stress-related triggers. I sent him to other specialists and hoped they would find something I couldn't see. I felt anxious seeing him on my schedule because while I thought he left feeling cared for, I never felt he left feeling helped. Those knot-in-my-stomach, pressure-in-my-head feelings that generally signal there is more to the story, in this case alerted me to this man's severe depression.

During the last couple of years, I dreaded seeing him in clinic. Although I knew he was not in control of his illness, I was frustrated and upset with him. Why couldn't he – why didn't he – take control and just get better? Of course I realized that my anger was really because I was unsuccessful in changing the course of his illness. We did discuss reasons to live, including his love of his wife and children. Once we talked about a prior suicide gesture and the impact it had on his children, who had become anxious and hyper-vigilant. "How can you even contemplate suicide?" I asked. In my mind, having children all but removed that choice from a menu of options. I struggled to control my feelings and to not convey judgment.

He swore, "I am not going to end my life. I just can't live with this pain. If you want me to live, take away my pain." Could I take away his pain? Medications, joint injections, other therapies when he could afford them had no reliable effect. His pain, believed by him to be specific to his muscles and joints, was to me the barometer of where he was with his psychiatric illness. Reflecting outside of our visits, I feared for his life. He had, in theory, the best psychiatric and medical care available, yet none of us had taken away his pain.

I received the page in the middle of a busy clinic. It was the lead psychiatrist from his team telling me that my patient had committed suicide. He had not kept an appointment, which was unlike him, and they requested a safety check that found him deceased. I was not really surprised by the news; in some ways it is numbing to fear a potential event for years. He was in his late forties when he took his life, and I was his doctor for most of the seven years before that.

I wonder: did I do enough for him? Could I have done more? I believe the answer is yes and yes, both answers contributing to the disquiet within me. His magnified and delusional guilt and self-loathing provided me with a lens for reflection about my own sense of guilt and inadequacy. Along with my sadness about his family's loss, I also had to recognize that my feelings were as much about my limitations as they were about him for threatening suicide and then carrying out his threat.

Doctoring gives me ample practice in exploring those ambiguous and shifting lines about responsibility and in approaching, at least, a compassionate place with myself. How is it that humans come to understand that maybe, just maybe, we are good enough? How many lessons that require self-assessment and then forgiveness must we have along the way towards that understanding and acceptance? All of our care did not keep him alive, but even when my efforts do not yield what I would want, even if my efforts fail, some days these are what we have: the effort, the even if, and the good enough.

The authors of the following stories face relationships with patients where they did not measure up to some standard and where the learning about themselves involves acknowledging their own frailties and limitations. Sometimes the lesson comes through our grappling with results of our work. Sometimes our patients model it. These are lessons of self-doubt, the effort of this work we do, and of self-acceptance, being good enough.

Help?
Stephanie Cooper

It was 3 AM, and the ER hallway reeked of alcohol and vomit accented by the subtle acrid waft of pus. In Bed A was a red-uniformed prisoner shackled to the frame, sent for "medical clearance" prior to booking at our county jail. "Medical clearance" meant the jail sent combative, restrained people to our ER to have us wrassle and hog-tie them and send some wide-eyed med student to poke their recalcitrant veins for blood. All of us were subject to the violence of the fight, as well as to the potential of Hepatitis B, Hepatitis C, HIV, TB, or simply spit and puke in the face.

In Bed B was an overweight Native American on a crack crash. Shipped to us by ambulance, she was delivered into a stinky hallway and summarily ignored. She was, per the nursing notes, combative on arrival and then somnolent as her cocaine high evaporated, leaving a leathery, worn mound of flesh wearing several layers of fetid clothing and snoring quietly. So very quietly, so imperceptibly faintly, that I had to grind my fist into her sternum to wake her and make sure she was still breathing and neurologically intact (so that she could linger in her liminal, public, substance-induced hibernation until she miraculously metabolized to freedom and the bear awoke and she roared to go).

Bed C was a man holding his right hand in bandages that were quickly turning from white to blood-red. He elevated it and watched the crowds of cops, med students, nurses, new patients delivered by ambulance, and old patients carted off or lumbering out on their own, the metronome of time ticking unsanitarily and loudly as he wondered if his fingers could and would be sewn back on or not. Nobody else seemed to know, and for hours prior to my arrival, apparently nobody had told him so.

Bed D was a crazed-looking man with a crooked but sweet smile and an Osama bin Laden beard. His blue and white Value Village shirt was besmirched with grime, and his dark eyes watched furtively as his body remained impassive and still. His face-sheet read "chest pain—known to have history of chronic chest pain (CP)." The patient was 38, appeared comfortable, not short of breath, not sweaty, not clutching his chest.

My doctor-manager mind, its creativity bludgeoned by years of acronyms and binary thinking, knew the plan for Bed D immediately. The plan was rote: Chest X-ray, EKG, troponin, chem. 7, aspirin by mouth, maybe GI cocktail for esophageal pain, then OTD, acronymese for Out The Door. Western medicine kicks you to the curb with a fancy three-letter blow.

The computer said this guy had been here with chest pain at least six times, and in all instances his blood-work, EKG, and chest X-ray were reassuring. Someone had recommended a GI scope, which he did not show up for. Others gave him loads of anti-ulcer medicines, little purple pill prescriptions, calling his symptoms "GERD," short for gastroesophageal reflux disease, or acid reflux.

Whatever, I thought. This guy is cuckoo, and we're not going to solve his problems in an ER hallway next to screaming prisoners and an almost-apneic crack mama. We're going to prove he doesn't have anything that will imminently kill him, and then we're going to send him OTD. Perhaps we in the ER say "OTD" instead of "home" because not even medicalese can bullshit that sending a homeless man back to the cold and loveless streets could qualify as "going home." Instead, the paperwork favors the euphemism, "discharged to self-care." Which of course assumes that said self is able to care for said self, as we, the medical establishment, clearly were not.

Paul, the med student on the case, presented Bed D to me. "Mr. X is a 38 year old man with frequent episodes of chest pain." Paul spelled out all the non-worrisome features—pain not worse with breathing, unchanged by exercise, no recent fever or cough. I felt my mental hot cocoa congeal into a cool scum.

"Okay," I interrupted, "So what do you want to do for him?"

Paul listed off the labs, EKG, X-ray that I had already decided upon before I'd heard a word about the patient.

"Good," I said. "If those are all normal, which they will be, then he goes."

Paul dutifully began to carry out the orders. In an hour or so, the blood work came back negative. The chest X ray was clear. The EKG was normal.

"So," I said, "OTD."

It was 3 AM, and the ambulances kept bringing in more patients now that the bars had closed. Assault to face with fists. Fall down eight stairs. Deformed hand after punching wall. The bodies were waiting for me, the attending physician, to see them.

Paul approached the coffee-cup strewn counter where I was voraciously charting. "But…," he began. I could hear the lip-biting hesitance in his voice, the pregnant pause.

I looked up at him. A preternaturally young, thin med student. Healthy looking. I recalled the time he was eating quinoa out of his Tupperware in the break room while I had cut slivers off ten donuts from Remo Borachini's Italian Bakery to sample every flavor. Then of course I had to "even out" the edges, sampling even more. "Do you eat quinoa in here to make the donut eaters guilty?" I chided.

Now he was looking at me, his dark pupils dilated by fatigue, in his blue, uncompromised irises. His corneas, clear and crystalline as a newborn baby's.

"I don't feel that we have HELPED him," Paul said.

Helped. Helped him. We haven't helped him. I tongued the words like insoluble gobstoppers. We hadn't helped the patient. Wait…wait a minute. I hadn't thought in those terms in months, if not years. Of course we should help the patient, but I mean really, people, this is an ER not a yoga therapy session.

"I mean, we haven't done anything to ease his pain," Paul said.

I was derailed, still choking on the word "helped." Of course we were supposed to – I was supposed to – help the patient. Isn't that why I signed up for this intellectual boot camp and endured those years of scholastic bulimia? to help other human beings?

But the game had changed. And the patients were gaming us, as well. Complaining of chest pain the moment they were arrested by the cops, or announcing they felt like killing themselves just when we told them they'd be discharged. The game had become management, throughput, with, yes, some appropriate elements of acting quickly to reduce pain quickly. But the game had also morphed into the reality that seeing more patients per hour translated into a productivity bonus.

The language became linked to money. Diagnosing "pharyngitis" billed $50 less than "acute pharyngitis" because "acute" made it seem to billers like more of an emergency. And while my English-major self loved the concept of ten dollars a letter (just like Vanna and Wheel of Fortune), my heart ached for the loss of innocence, for the loss of language not yoked to a cash cow.

The guy in Bed D wasn't ever a story to me. He was an exercise, a mathematical equation (CP = CXR, EKG, CBC, M7, troponin) solved in a nanosecond, a reflex. Had I become such a sycophant of the system that I didn't even see health care in terms of healing anymore?

Paul was waiting for my answer as I was having an existential meltdown in the hallway of Zone 4, my head canted slightly to the right, my mind repeating, "but we haven't helped him…. Helped him."

"You know," I emerged from the existential quagmire, "You are right. We haven't helped him. Not at all. We've drawn his blood and poked him, and the nurses'll give you an 'Atta boy!' when you discharge him to his self-care home of the street, but no, Paul, we haven't helped him.

What would you like to do to help him?" I asked, sincere.

His baby-clear corneas glinted in the incandescence. "You know, I think the only way that we can help these people is by listening to them, listening to their stories. Sometimes we are the only people they have to talk to, and sometimes we are the only ones who really care."

He was right.

Paul went back to talk more to the patient in Bed D.

Amy, the long-time ER nurse, and I stood in silence. "Help people?" said Amy. "What a concept."

"I knew my compassion had evaporated somewhat," I admitted, "but I didn't realize all I had left in the cup was salt!"

The ambulance company had dropped off four more patients. The guy with the amputated fingers' bandage was now solid red, not a speck of white left. "Helped him…Helped…" the words wrangled in my mouth like tapioca pearls, as I tried to collect them so as to avoid swallowing them. "Amy," I said, "I think I'm having an existential moment," wondering how she'd console or counsel.

"C'mon, they're 4th-year med students—they'll get over it."

Is compassion just some idea, like freedom, used as political capital to sell the violence of western medicine? Pablum to armor ourselves with to get us through the process, only to find that, debt-laden and mind-washed on the other side of the world from where we began, there is no real reward – no oil or glory for the soldiers, and no healing or helping in our health care?

Frozen in the hallway at 3:15 AM I knew I should go sternal-rub Bed B and lean on orthopedics to get the finger amps to the OR, should go hear report on the new patients and dispo the red-robed prisoner back to jail, but I just stood there a few moments longer.

Missing the Mark
Sharon Dobie

We had never met. He was on my schedule for an acute problem, some-thing about congestion, which should make for a quick visit, or so I thought. There was no recent history to review, because his chart indicated that he had not been seen in our clinic in the previous two years. Since he was a 40 year-old man, I hoped and presumed he had a good chance of being fairly healthy. Presumption: usually a bad idea.

Despite the patient down the hall, now with a IV in her arm, getting intravenous fluids to stave off a trip to the emergency room for dehydra-tion from a bad flu attack, and despite the patient for whom an intrauterine device placement was complicated and her visit lengthened by her fainting, I was only 20 minutes behind and was sure (another assumption) that I could catch up with this guy with sniffles. Odds were, I told myself with a little un-warranted cockiness, he did not even need to be seeing a doctor for a cold.

"What brings you in today?" was my standard opening. I hoped my face did not visibly fall when he said, "I've got a list of things. I've not been to the doctor in a number of years and ya know, things build up. I'm getting older and that worries me." Often, maybe even usually, I will then ask the patient to tell me the list, not the details, just the list. In case we don't have time to address everything, I'll ask what the most important items are before getting the details about each concern. As part of that conversation I weigh in if anything I have heard strikes me as really needing to jump to the top of the list. I don't want to reach the end of a visit where we've spent all our time on the skin rash that concerns the patient and we've not considered some really major symptom or exam finding such as chest pain or an ab-dominal mass.

For some reason that day, I reversed the order and did not get the list first. "Well," I said, "we only have fifteen minutes, so we'll need to figure out together what we can cover today and what we can address at a future visit."

"But I wanted a full physical. I waited two weeks for this appointment. Everything on my list is important."

"Everything on your list is important," I tried to reassure him, "but you are scheduled in a 15-minute appointment to take care of a quick, acute problem."

"That is not my fault. Yes I have a cough now and have been having chills. But my back is also acting up and I can't lift anything. And there is so much stress that I am not sleeping and I have to keep looking for work. The headaches stop me dead in my tracks. And my father died of a heart attack at 42. I don't know what my cholesterol is or if I should be worried about my hemorrhoids. We may lose our house."

I was close to hyperventilating at that moment. And I was mentally trying to see some way around all this, maybe through some of it. "Each and every one of these issues deserves time. Today let's see what we can do to get them sorted and start evaluating. I promise you we will make headway in the time we have left."

"No!" he almost yelled at me and then I saw that he was close to tears. "I have to deal with these things now. My life is falling apart. I think we are going to lose our house. My wife and I are fighting all the time. And I wonder if I am dying."

By now we had used up most of our time. I had two choices. One was to push on, do what I could, start an evaluation I could not finish, and let him leave angry, sad, and dissatisfied. I wouldn't recoup any of the minutes I was already behind, and later patients would be irritated for being kept waiting, but I would not be any further behind. Or I could take a deep breath, admit I had blown the encounter from the beginning, and start over. That would probably mean spending more than 40 minutes with the patient, and my waiting patients might transition from irritated to irate.

Had I entered the room with a focus on my patient, rather than on the math of being "on time" or "behind," I might have heard his initial comments differently, adding in data that was right before my eyes: his difficulty making eye contact at first, the unsmiling countenance, his unanimated speech. Fully eliciting what he wanted to discuss before closing him off with my parameters might have put us in a better position from which to start working together.

We face competing expectations all the time. Be there for our patient. Meet their needs. Don't miss anything serious. Tend to the person. Be on time. Don't keep anyone waiting. Be responsive to emails, phone calls, prescription refills, requests to squeeze another patient into the schedule. Get charting completed. Answer pages.

Be open-ended, yet get finished on time seem to be the two sides of the coin between which I live much of my clinical life. Getting trapped by letting the pendulum swing too far is common. If I veer towards efficiency, trusting my rapid perceptions and the early information I gather, I am at risk for an encounter like the one above: derailed before we have even started. If I relax into the unbounded space of my more loquacious patients, I will fall hopelessly behind, and as the day progresses, I will face the increasing criticism of my remaining patients. Caught up in the attempt to get it right, I sometimes don't even know if I actually connected or was just getting it right.

On that particular day I chose to stop, acknowledge our rocky start, and ask to start over, this time really listening to what was on his mind. I stepped out first to ask that my next few patients be advised that I was going to be running even later than they had expected. When he and I started again, we were able to begin an evaluation and treatment of both his physical and emotional concerns.

In that nanosecond between his eruption of anger at me and my decision about how to manage, I was a bit horrified. What I observed in the quick replay of the prior eight minutes was a robot, efficient and even smart, but a robot nonetheless. It was not a person, not a physician. And I was not pleased with myself.

Patient Caregiver

Anonymous

As a medical student and now as a resident, I've found the public perception that doctors think they are infallible to be unbelievable. When you are in training, at times it feels like you don't know anything.

As an intern on the family medicine ward service, I was pretty beaten down by the first half of a difficult year. My confidence was shaky, and I was exhausted. The holidays were coming, and I was not looking forward to missing my family's celebration because of being on call. In the midst of all this, though, I was very excited about my first continuity obstetrics patient. I had been following L.T. for the latter part of her second pregnancy along with one of our faculty doctors. She was L.T.'s primary care provider (PCP) and had known her for years. L.T. had developed some complications late in her pregnancy that required some extra testing and monitoring, and that generated a whole lot more stress and anxiety for her and her husband, and perhaps for me to some degree. After several false alarms and a failed induction, she finally came to the hospital in active labor on December 15.

As can often be the case in labor and delivery, tension was running high. The pregnancy complications and failed induction were on everyone's mind. L.T.'s labor was progressing, but slowly, and she received medications to augment it. Having my very first continuity obstetrics patient while I was the intern on the service made me feel like a real doctor. L.T. was looking to me for answers! This rarely happens to an intern—people generally look to you for things like replacing electrolytes, calling for test results, and performing various other low-level tasks. I did a cervical exam to see if her cervix had dilated or thinned out any more with the boost of the oxytocin drip. Her cervix was 6 cm dilated, which reassured her since it showed progress. My attending (her PCP) rechecked her cervix shortly later, and noted that she was still only 4 cm. I was standing next to L.T. when her PCP said this. L. looked at me immediately, but not with the recrimination that I expected, the recrimination that is an intern's alter ego. She looked concerned—about me. Concerned about me, during the middle of a difficult labor.

We left the room, and I returned later to check on her. I apologized for the mistake. "Don't worry!" she said. "Last time, two of the doctors disagreed about my exam as well. That exam can't be very precise." At the time, I was grateful for her kindness, and moved on quickly to other work. It wasn't until later that I felt utterly, completely, and maybe pathetically grateful to her, not just for her kindness but also for her ... mercy, for lack of a better word.

Now as a third-year resident, I wish I could say that was the end of any self-critical inner monologue, a phenomenon that is insidious in medicine (which, ironically, may lead to the paradoxical public perception of the opposite). I certainly didn't shed it that day. But at that moment, I felt that I was more than just my mistake.

Mental Calculus
Keisa Fallin-Bennett

The worst thing I ever did to a patient during the course of my residency became completely clear to me just after I left the clinic. In the midst of the commute home after that long typical day, I was frantically scribbling new scenarios of how the encounter should have happened, when clarity hit me: I had just enabled one of my patients to possibly harm herself, and there was nothing I could do now to fix it.

Reina was not one of the patients who had immediately stood out as "difficult." Perhaps she had initially presented for a touch of hypertension or insomnia. But as time went on, her story emerged: abuse and neglect suffered as a child, and later her husband and daughter, her only family in this country, left her. Her attempts to reconcile with her daughter had been met only with coldness. Over the years she had self-medicated with drugs and alcohol, and self-neglect. She had been hospitalized multiple times and finally admitted that she still heard the hallucinatory voices almost daily, but that she couldn't say this in public or she would be locked up in that horrible mental hospital again.

The day I can't forget occurred after she had seemed to be better for a month or so. She was tearful when I walked into the room, but was hesitant to talk. Finally, in a trembling voice, she managed to tell me about her true "chief complaint."

"I just heard that my grandmother died back in my country. She raised me and I need to go to the funeral, but don't have any money for a plane ticket." After sobbing quietly for a few minutes, she dropped her gaze to the floor and almost whispering, she asked, "I feel so embarrassed to ask you this, but can you loan me $50 for part of the ticket? I'll pay you back as soon as I can."

My mental calculus immediately ruled out a loan; I knew our unequal power relationship meant that being owed money wouldn't be ethical. But a small gift that I could advise her to pay forward to another person some day didn't raise any immediate red flags. So after some appropriate expressions of sympathy, I handed her the $20 I had in my wallet as a contribution.

It was only in the car, away from other distractions, on my way home, that the feeling of wrongness emerged. I suddenly realized that the whole story could very well be a lie, that she could be using the $20 to buy cocaine or some other source of self-harm. Not only that, but I realized even though I did not loan her the money, I had engaged the classic pharmaceutical rep trick. They show up in our offices, offer gifts or lunch, and subtly we feel we owe them to buy their product. My gift to her also imposed a psychic and emotional debt she now owed me. Also, I knew better than to trust her. She had a severe psychiatric illness and admitted addiction problems. My stomach was unsettled, and I felt like I was the one who was ill.

During the commute I realized my mistake, but it took months for me to admit the feelings I had that day were anger, disappointment, and shame, directed at both her and myself. Was it because I had wanted to be liked, even by someone whose admiration and gratitude would so likely be transient? Had I not learned that true compassion sometimes means saying no? Did I just feel so impotent to solve her health problems that I had to "fix" something, however ill-advised?

Years later I still ask myself these questions, and with surprise, notice that I don't remember if I saw her again or ever knew what she did with the $20. I have reconciled with myself that it is unlikely this "gift" did any major damage to her. But the real gift was my re-acquaintance with my feelings, intuition, and ability to recognize when mental calculus is inadequate or even wrong. Sometimes just witnessing, even just witnessing my own story, is enough.

Someone of Value

Christina Tanner

I was a new internal medicine resident on my second rotation, the Medical Intensive Care Unit, and I was tired, grumpy, and nervous. There were just two of us on this month-long rotation: 28 hours of call on, 20 hours off, day after day. At some time during the second or third week, I was called down to the emergency room to admit a sick elderly gentleman. He was there with his wife, in the bed by the wall, in a narrow room separated by a wisp of curtain from other frail, multiply monitored and intubated patients. The couple was polite, gracious, and elegant, even in their pain and fear. I asked the usual questions, did the usual exam, and wrote the usual orders. I don't remember what he had or how he fared, but I do know he made it out of the ICU, because as it turned out, he was a friend of Barbara, my mother-in-law.

Several months after his hospitalization, at a social gathering, in casual conversation with Barbara, he happened to mention that I had seen him in the ER and had admitted him. His wife apparently said: "She was like an angel." What my angelic qualities were, I do not know. Me, in my crumpled lab coat and scrubs, my running shoes and ponytail. I hope I was kind and caring and friendly and interested. Just normal. I hope I answered some questions, alleviated some fears.

Every June now, for more than ten years, I hear a predictable complaint from our senior residents: "I can't believe the front desk scheduled me with a new patient! Don't they know that I'm graduating in two weeks? What am I supposed to tell the patient? 'Sure I can see you today, but that's all. I'm leaving, I'm gone.' How fair is that?"

I say: "No. You're looking at this the wrong way. You have a great opportunity here. You have no idea how powerful an impact you might have on this patient. Even in one visit. Even just by listening. Even just by being you. But that's not all. Someday, you will not believe how powerful an impact that patient will have on you, should you ever hear of the visit from their point of view." Just as I did those years ago, when that charming elderly couple taught me, a shy and insecure resident, that I had something of value to offer.

Cancer After All

Anonymous

I don't know if it is a cultural phenomenon, a personality clash, or more likely a combination of both, but I am truly overwhelmed by this Russian couple. They catastrophize everything. Instead of describing a symptom like "I have a headache or I have chest pain," they say, "Doctor, I don't know what is wrong with me; you must figure out what is wrong with me. There is something wrong with my heart, my head, and my… Sometimes I just die for a little bit and then I get better. My body just stops working. Tell me what's wrong. You need to do tests and figure out what's wrong with me."

I have been caring for Mr. and Mrs. S for several years. They are well-educated individuals, and in their country they pursued professional careers, he as an engineer and she as a teacher. In this country, however, they work as janitors. They are not yet eligible for retirement, but they tell me they are too tired and too old to keep doing this manual labor. They beg me to find a way to claim they are disabled so they won't have to work anymore. They see "disability" as their only option, because they don't have enough income currently to just stop working.

Mrs. S always has downcast, sad eyes, cries easily, peppers me with rapid-fire questions, and pleads with me to tell her what is wrong. Mr. S is slightly less anxious, but his questions are as insistent as his wife's. Each time they come in, they have so many symptoms and concerns that a 20-minute visit inevitably stretches into 40-60 minutes despite all my attempts to set an agenda. Although their English is superficially good, we don't truly understand one another most of the time. I request an interpreter but they refuse to work with one, further complicating our interactions. With the cultural, personality, financial, and language issues, every visit with them is emotionally and physically challenging for me.

When I try to ask questions to help focus their concerns, I am bombarded. They report a significant problem in response to each question I ask, what we call a "pan-positive" review of symptoms. It seems like every inch of their bodies is suffering from some major ailment. "Doctor, of course I also have problems with my vision and my mouth hurts, I can't breathe well, I have stomach pains, my joints ache, I have this rash." etc. etc. etc. My attempts to clarify their concerns only end up creating even more confusion, and I feel like giving up. I keep trying to redirect the conversation, but I cannot get a word in edgewise. "Doctor, I also have this pain in my leg, oh yeah, and my heart hurts…"

I can feel my own heart racing and I begin to feel defeated. I look at the clock and I know that I will be behind for the rest of my clinic day. In my gut I know many of their concerns can be explained by their anxiety and desperation to find a solution to their social stressors, but since I cannot create a comprehensive story, I never quite trust my judgment. They are convinced that if I just did more "tests" I would be able to finally give them "the answer" they seek. At every visit they beg me to do an X-Ray of their whole body to look for what is wrong, to check some more blood tests, and to maybe order a scope of their intestines. At first, since I never felt very clear about their histories, I would obtain blood tests and imaging studies to try and make us all feel better. The results were always normal, which, not surprisingly, never satisfied my patients' quest for an answer.

Then I changed tactics and laboriously explained why I could not order every requested test at every visit. Instead, I requested their help to try and focus on just one or two issues each time. I heard myself say over and over "I cannot keep ordering things just so we don't miss anything." I moved from practicing defensively and ordering a bunch of tests to cover my butt, to actually erring on the side of less evaluation, thinking this was likely in their best interest. Of course, in the back of my mind I kept worrying "what if I do miss something?"

A couple of months ago, Mr. S saw one of my colleagues on a day I wasn't available. He described having problems swallowing. She sent him for endoscopy, where the gastroenterologist looked down his esophagus with a scope. They diagnosed him with stage IV esophageal cancer. I think that he and his wife believe that they told me about this symptom before. With the flood of symptoms I tried to tackle in each visit, it is certainly possible that they mentioned a swallowing problem at some point. I cannot recollect it and it is not in my chart notes. They weren't mad at me (or at least they never said), but I felt awful. Was this my fault? Should I have done something differently? Had I stopped really listening to them?

I have such mixed emotions about my relationship with this couple. I really like them and I want to care for them. At the same time, whenever I see their names on my patient list for the day my heart starts racing, I feel stressed out and at times I want to scream "God, not again. I can't take it anymore."

I recently saw Mrs. S in clinic after she learned about her husband's diagnosis. Of course, she wants me to test and scan her for "everything." I understand her fear and anxiety, but I still don't believe that's the appropriate thing to do. Unfortunately, my discussions about not testing for everything, just in case, are now ineffective; I imagine that she believes we would have detected her husband's cancer earlier had I tested him this way in the first place. I feel like I'm beating my head against the wall.

At her last visit, I spent over an hour with her and we got nowhere. I left mid-appointment and ran into a colleague in the hall and started crying. I was feeling sad about the whole situation, but also angry. The amount of energy it took to work with this couple was killing me, and despite all my attempts to utilize good communication skills, I couldn't get anywhere. But pulling myself together, I went back into the room to finish the appointment. I don't know if Mrs. S noticed my red, puffy eyes, but she launched right back into describing her numerous symptoms. When I left clinic that day and arrived home I broke down again. How could I keep this up?

I haven't seen her in clinic since this last visit and I am afraid of how I'll respond when I do. How do I balance my desire to be empathetic and supportive with my own mental health needs? I've thought about this for months. If I get too sucked in, I lose balance and swing in the other direction, avoiding connection and empathy. I am trying to become more mindful of my visceral responses and use them as a trigger to take a step back and look differently at the relationship and the current needs of my patient. What are appropriate goals and expectations for this visit and this relationship? When have I gotten to the point that I am no longer objective enough to appropriately care for certain patients? What buttons are these clinical interactions pushing in me, and are these the same "buttons" that I have in my personal life?

When I can step back and try to answer these questions, I recognize these challenging situations as learning moments. I am learning to take more deep breaths, to slow down my heart rate and try to remember this couple does not know what my buttons are, so how can they avoid them? Working with them helped me develop the skill of being mindful of the emotions brought up in me; I have learned more about myself. This doesn't mean it's going to be easy, but I am hoping that this insight will make this relationship sustainable and that I carry it into future relationships in and out of work.

Acceptance
Sharon Dobie

"I love that boy. He is a great kid," said Mr. D.

These words came after a discussion of his "code status" and whom we should call if we needed to call family. The "great kid" was a 50-year-old man who lived several blocks away from him and likely looked in on him every day. This man was not the son Mr. D would want us to call.

He first identified his oldest son Jack and gave us his number. When we asked if we should also have the phone number of his son who lived across the street, he said, "Naw, Pete is kind of laid back, but my grandson Marcus, you should call him. Marcus is like his Uncle Jack. Marcus' dad was killed in a tragic accident soon after he and Marcus' mom were married. He never knew his dad. He is a great kid." Marcus is married and has children.

"Jack is a retired army officer, same as me. Pete had a full time job and was laid off. Now he works part time at Jack in the Box. I have kids at both ends. I love 'em both."

At 87, sitting there in the ED, oxygen going into his nose, with pneumonia, Mr. D chuckled as he talked about his youngest son. "His mother was always on him to make more of himself. I knew that was not him and tried to get her to lay off a bit. He has three storage units and so much stuff in his house, I can't go over there any more. He is a kind and wonderful person."

Acceptance: 10PM, sitting in the emergency room, a reminder provided by Mr. D. unknowingly. In his mind, he was there because he was ill and needed our intravenous fluids and antibiotics and a day or two in a hospital bed. In my mind, he was also a role model for tolerance and acceptance.

Adios

Sharon Dobie

Many years ago George Harvey provided me with a lasting visual reminder of several lessons. There is not too much to tell about him. He was
a favorite patient of mine in residency, in his early fifties, a tall, overweight
man who lived from welfare check to welfare check, in the Fillmore district
of San Francisco, probably in substandard housing. He was also a heroin addict. Occasionally I would see him in clinic; just as often he was a no-show.

"Hi, George. How are things? What brings you in today?" I might ask,
if he did show up for an appointment, to which he would respond, "How
are YOU doing, Doc? You look really beat. You're working too hard. You
need to take it easy."

The next steps in our routine usually were about his blood pressure and
whether he was taking his medications, how much intravenous heroin he
was using, and how he was feeling overall. He used somewhat sporadically.
When he was not using, he took his medications, kept appointments, even
looked for work. When he was using, I would not see him for months.

Later that first intern year, George started having chest pains and I
developed a real taste for worry. With George, I worried about endocarditis,
an infection of the heart valves that IV heroin users can get, and I worried
that he would have a heart attack. He was certainly at risk for endocarditis.
He was also at risk for the heart attack because he was an overweight,
African American man with high blood pressure. Over several months we
admitted him to the hospital four or five times. While we did the tests to
prove he did not have an infection of his heart valves or a blockage in
his coronary arteries, he and I had long chats about his options to enter a
recovery program.

"Yeah, I'll think about it, Doc," he would reassure me. "All this is leading to no good. Time to do something, I can see." I really believed I was
going to be instrumental in changing this man's life.

One day, as I walked to the hospital from my car, planning the conversation we would have that day when I visited him, I looked up as the city bus

went by. There in the bus window was George, dressed, standing and holding on to the bus rail with one hand and with the other, holding his IV bag up. Our eyes met, he smiled and waved. I never saw him again.

Epilogue
Our stories and the ethics of writing about patients

Sharon Dobie

Sitting in a coffee shop, I anxiously awaited one of my patients. I invited him to meet with me to read the story I wrote about what I learned from our working together over a period of more than 15 years. As editor and author, I was preparing to submit the manuscript for *Heart Murmurs: What Patients Teach Their Doctors*. All of the stories deserve permission from the patients described in the book; fewer than half could be reached to ask for this permission.

Some contacts were easy. There is a chapter on those whose cheery dispositions brighten our days in clinic. When I met with them and family members, they enjoyed that I wrote about them in this way. But what about the more challenging lessons? This was the concern as I waited that day in the coffee shop. His was a difficult story, a past experience for him, and a lasting lesson for me. I wondered if he would veto it being in the book. After arriving and chatting, he read what I had written. I sat there sweating, and then he said he liked it. He offered some ideas for changing the details that blinded the story, adding, "I remember that visit, and it is really interesting to see how you saw it, because for me it was similar and different at the same time."

This is how all these meetings have gone: I am anxious and worried and our patients are gracious and grateful for the project, touched that they have taught us and we are willing to describe those lessons.

Reviewing stories with the individuals represented in them adds value to the relationships we have. One family member of a person who is deceased agreed with my perceptions and contributed details that were important and ultimately enriched the story. Several commented on how the story was accurate but that I left out details that were important to them. Sometimes those had to do with what I did for them (much of which I do not remember, and of course is not the purpose of this book). When reading a difficult story, several reached out to reassure me or another author. Each of the reviews went well, validating the project and our perceptions of these patient-doctor relationships.

Our physician authors reviewed their narratives as we approached publication; for many this occurred a number of years after they wrote their stories. Older and more experienced, several commented that the revisit was a reminder of how they thought earlier in their career. They could see how they have changed as well as the characteristics that remain.

I remain uncertain of how to get the ethics of patient protection right. I do believe that when we meet with patients and have conversation about a written narrative, the relationship grows. Doctors have written about their patients for centuries. Most of those writings, until very recently, spoke to a culture where the patient was less of an equal partner in the physician-patient equation than what we currently believe and teach. Certainly, most of those years also preceded current privacy regulations. As recently as fifteen years ago, this subject was not routinely scrutinized. I have no idea where it will be ten years from now.

The emerging ethic about writing about our patients is not well defined. What can we say? What should we not say? Can we even do this writing? Memoirs tell only one person's perceptions. What should determine how a physician addresses this? In prior works, names and circumstances might be changed, but is that enough? Is there a different line when we are writing the story about a relationship defined by confidentiality? At the very least, these are muddy waters.

In *Heart Murmurs*, the authors wrote about what they learned about themselves because of and within a relationship with a patient. We can't tell that story without the story of the patient. How then do we protect the covenant of confidentiality? Today I sit with a manuscript with more than thirty authors and many stories of mine. Where I am settling, and where I hope it is good for the mores of today, is the following:

All stories must meet several criteria:

The value of telling the story is important to our social dialogue. The purpose of this project is one that meets this criteria for all the narratives included here.

The story is told in a respectful way for each person represented. In this book, all stories, even those that have difficult circumstances, are respectful.

If a person believes a story is about them, they should not feel embarrassed or shamed.

At the same time that I use these criteria, I recognize the subjectivity and bias inherent in them. All stories include names and often some circumstances that have been altered, except for two where family explicitly approved using the actual name. Patients of mine either read their piece, or they are deceased and I couldn't find a family member for review, or the piece is a composite, or it is about persons with whom I worked many years ago and I could not find them.

If a physician contributor wanted to attach their name to their story one of the following criteria had to be be met:

The author shared the narrative with their patient and the patient agreed to it being published; or

The patient is deceased and the author shared it with a family member who agreed that it can be published; or

The patient is deceased and no family member is easily found or reachable and the story is generic enough that the identity seems reasonably protected; or

The story is a composite and thus not attributable to one person; or

The story is from a number of years ago and no one could be contacted and it is blinded enough so that identity seems reasonably protected from any but possibly the patient.

If one of these criteria was not met, a story will be "anonymous" and the author may have a biographical note if they wish. For stories with an anonymous author and with the authors being from all over the country, I believe patients' identities are reasonably protected. Even if a person or a family member reads the book and identifies with the circumstances in a story and wonders if it is about them, their identity should be protected from others. What I know: the lessons in every narrative in this book have been experienced in one way or another by every author who contributed, and widely by all of us, be we patients or physicians.

Authors' Biographical Notes

Chad Abbott MD, MPH was a student of life long before he was a student of medicine. He was the first generation of his family to attend college and directly after his graduation from San Diego State University with an undergraduate degree in biology, he found himself in the role of caregiver to his father who was suffering from chronic liver disease. His father's death was a poignant experience and inspired Chad (against the odds) to pursue a career as a physician.

Chad entered Tulane Medical School at the age of 30, older than most of his classmates, but equipped with life lessons that most younger people had not yet experienced.

He is constantly reminded that he is not just educating his patients, but that they are educating him. Each person carries with them stories about their home, job, stress, relationships, beliefs, education and general outlook on life and every time he works with a patient, he is challenged and awed by their stories and perseverance.

In addition to focusing on individual patients he also focuses on public and population health. While at Tulane he received his Masters in Public Health. This allows him to see the greater picture, including the social, political and economic determinants of health. He also learned that teaching in the community is a great way to help individuals improve their health. He also enjoys this endeavor immensely.

Most important to Dr. Abbott is to be a lifelong student of medicine and life in general. He feels tremendously lucky to have found a career that provides not only the impetus, but also the opportunity to continue to learn every day.

Richard Arnold MD is particularly interested in how medical teachers can influence the choices made by trainees and help them hang on to the ideals that brought them to a life of service. He went to medical school and completed his residency in Chicago, Illinois, followed by several years in south-east Asia that opened his eyes to the powerful role of culture in our opinions and perspectives. At the University of Washington School of Medicine, he now spends half his time as a Clinical Professor of Medicine and primary care internist and the other half as Head of the Snake River College where he teaches and mentors medical students while teaching them clinical skills.

Irf Asif MD finds the relationship built between a patient and physician to be the most personally challenging yet satisfying aspect of medicine. He believes physicians can prescribe or advocate, but optimal outcomes require time spent looking through the patient's eyes. For him, primary care and sports medicine bring a blend of experiences and knowledge for active individuals to connect with and utilize. He is from Ohio and completed his undergraduate training at Xavier University, medical school at the University of Cincinnati, and Family Medicine/Sports Medicine Fellowship at the University of Washington.

Currently he is the Vice Chair of Academics & Research, Primary Care Sports Medicine Fellowship Director, and Associate Professor in the Greenville Health System/University of South Carolina-Greenville Medical School Department of Family Medicine. He lives with his wife, Sonia, who practices veterinary ophthalmology. Sometimes, he thinks her experiences of seeing the eyes of bears, lions, tigers, bald eagles, horses, dogs, cats, and turtles exceed his own experiences. At least it makes for wonderful dinner conversation each evening.

He enjoys research and educating young physicians. As an expert in the field of sports cardiology, he has been invited to speak at a number of venues, including the International Olympic Committee Conference on Injury Prevention

Keisa Fallin-Bennett MD, MPH is an assistant professor in the Department of Family and Community Medicine at the University of Kentucky, Lexington, Kentucky where she participates in clinical care, teaching, and research in health services. She earned an MD and Masters in Public Health at the University of Kentucky, completed residency in Lawrence Massachusetts in 2008, and the Primary Care Policy Fellowship at Georgetown University and the Robert Graham Center in 2009. Her research focuses on the relationship of lesbian, gay, bisexual and transgender social networks and smoking behavior in Appalachia. She is the co-chair of the Group on LGBT Health of the Society of Teachers of Family Medicine.

Melanie Parker Berg MD practices family medicine with obstetrics in the southern Puget Sound region with Group Health Cooperative in Puyallup, Washington. She resides in the town of Ruston with her husband and baby girl, where they enjoy stroller walks and sailing around the Sound. Her piece was written during residency.

Throughout his career, **Ted Carter MD** has maintained an interest in teaching, medical ethics, and the philosophy of the practice of medicine. He did his residency in pediatrics at Walter Reed Army Medical Center and then spent the next 20 years in military medicine followed by 10 years at the University of Washington/Seattle Children's Hospital. He then moved to Phoenix to be closer to his family. He specializes in pediatric pulmonary medicine as Chief, Division of Pulmonary and Sleep Medicine at Banner Children's Specialists, Mesa, Arizona, and Clinical Professor of Pediatrics, University of Arizona College of Medicine.

Kavitha Chunchu MD grew up in Virginia. She obtained her medical degree through the Medical College of Virginia. She made the big leap to the west coast by completing her Family Medicine residency at the University of Washington and is currently practicing family medicine in The Everett Clinic, a multi specialty group in Snohomish County, Washington. In her free time she enjoys kayaking, reading, and getting into adventures and misadventures in the US and abroad.

Prior to his untimely passing in 2010, **Mitchell Cohen MD** practiced full spectrum rural family medicine in Elma, Washington. Mitch enjoyed teaching the next generation of physicians and writing about the non-medical aspects of medicine. A graduate of Loyola University Stritch School of Medicine, Mitch was adjunct clinical faculty at the University of Washington School of Medicine and part time faculty at St. Peter Hospital. With a passion for rural medicine and dedication to "womb to tomb" care, Mitch enjoyed making house calls and touched many lives with his kind and generous spirit. Above all, Mitch was a devoted husband and loving father to his three children and is missed by his patients, friends, and family.

Stephanie Cooper MD, MS is an emergency medicine physician in Seattle, Washington, where she lives with her partner and twin sons. Stephanie is deeply committed to the practice of narrative medicine—medicine infused with the act of telling and listening to stories. In addition to prioritizing the patient's story and how people make meaning of their lived experiences with illness and wellness, she recognizes the importance of eliciting and valuing the stories of healthcare providers. Stephanie believes that reflection is essential for providers to maintain the compassion and humanity that drew them to medicine in the first place. Towards that end, she teaches narrative medicine and biomedical ethics courses that provide sanctioned space for students to engage in these key elements of the informal curriculum.

Sharon Dobie MD, MCP is a die-hard generalist who believes foremost in the strength of human relationships. She started out as an American Studies major then morphed into city planning with a multidisciplinary approach to social policy planning. From there she moved on to medicine, always certain family medicine was the most appropriate specialty for working with the underserved. She also knew it would protect her from boredom. She augments her full clinical practice by adding more variety through doing what she hopes is policy relevant research, teaching medical students and residents, supporting students to be engaged in community service and health equity initiatives, and mentoring anyone who will listen to her or swim with her in the lake. This project came to be because of all of the living she has shared and continues to share with her patients, friends, and family. She is a Professor of Family Medicine at the University of Washington, in Seattle, where she lives and where her adult sons often visit, sometimes for extended stays as a roommate. This is her first book-length project.

Sara Ehdaie DO is an Osteopathic family physician at Legacy Community Health Services and a full time faculty member at the Houston Methodist San Jacinto Family Medicine Residency Program, Baytown Texas, where she thoroughly enjoys teaching residents and medical students. She has a special interest in arthritis and musculoskeletal medicine. After much research, she continues to believe that laughter and finding ways to encourage movement are the best medicines. In her time off, she enjoys exploring nature and reading books on philosophy, education, and the Hitchhiker's Guide to the Galaxy.

Claudia Finkelstein MDCM is a general internist who has practiced medicine in many different settings since graduating from McGill University Medical School in Montreal, Quebec, Canada in 1986. In each setting she has loved caring for and getting to know patients and their incredible stories. She is a Clinical Associate Professor of Medicine at the University of Washington, Seattle, Washington. She loves learning along with her students, residents, and colleagues and is extremely grateful to have been allowed to be a part of and witness to so many lives. She is the mother of two splendid young adult women. She loves to read, write, and run and wishes there were more hours in every day; then perhaps she could finally perfect the ideal home made pie crust.

Jessie Fudge MD currently lives near Seattle, Washington and works as a sports medicine physician (Activity Sport and Exercise Medicine) with Group Health Cooperative in Everett, Washington. Having grown up in Minnesota, she loves the cold and even spent some time working in Antarctica. Outside of work, she enjoys skiing, traveling and spending time with family.

Kelly Gabler MD is a Family Physician from Houston, Texas. She received her undergraduate degree in Biology from Loyola University, New Orleans, and then returned to Texas for medical training. She graduated from the University of Texas Medical School in Houston and completed her residency training at the Memorial Family Medicine Residency Program in Southwest Houston. She became fluent in medical Spanish through her work with diverse patient populations and her medical mission trips to coastal Ecuador. She is an active member of the Texas Academy of Family Physicians and the local Harris County chapter. At the San Jacinto Campus of Legacy Community Health Services, in Baytown, Texas, she has coordinated grant-sponsored free mammograms for uninsured patients and worked to enhance resident education in geriatric medicine and nursing home care. In her free time she enjoys cooking, gardening, salt water fishing, playing with her dog, and spending time with family and friends.

Kelley Glancey MD is a family physician who now also has twins of her own. She is married and working on change and growth in her marriage everyday. She went to medical school at George Washington University followed by residency at the University of Washington. Currently she works in a two physician micro practice in Winter Park, Colorado with her Dad where she is not only a doctor but also a secretary, biller and nurse.

Sarah Hale MD wrote her essay during residency and currently practices full spectrum family medicine. Although her work is mostly in an outpatient clinic, she also delivers babies, takes care of patients in the hospital, and works with residents. She has worked in a rural practice, and in urban and academic settings. She appreciated this project of writing down and sharing a meaningful patient experience. Outside of work, she enjoys reading, spending time with friends and family, and exploring the area where she lives, whether hiking, running, bicycling, or trying a new restaurant.

As a kid **Sarah Hufbauer MD** says she "wanted to know, understand, and help underdogs. At that time, and in that place in Southern California, that meant animals, Latinos, poor folks." In her words:

"Later I gave up on people and wanted to just focus on helping animals. After a teenage year in Denmark, my belief returned that humans were salvageable and worth fighting for. My experience at Swarthmore College heightened my sense of justice and deepened my sense of the complexity of human interaction and power structures. Time in Mexico and Guatemala honed my sense of adventure and appreciation for the beauty and difficulty of reaching over into new cultures.

"Medical school at UC Irvine settled me into Family Medicine as the way to make all these connections and use my privilege for good. Group Health Cooperative's residency reinforced the notion that a community is only healthy when all individuals are offered opportunities to reach their potentials. Working for 20 years as a staff physician and now Clinical Site Director at Country Doctor Community Health Centers, an urban community clinic in Seattle, has been richly challenging. Patients so unlike me are teaching me every day about themselves, about my perceptions and assumptions, about the ability to connect across difference. My piece here is an offering to the insights and difficult lessons my patients and I have shared."

Ahalya Joisha MD grew up in India, in a family of physicians. After completing medical school at the Kasturba Medical College in India, she moved to Seattle for her family medicine residency at the Group Health Cooperative. She then pursued a career in geriatrics, completing fellowship training in the Stanford-VA Geriatrics Fellowship Program. Currently she works as a geriatrician at the San Mateo County Hospital's Ron Robinson Senior Center and as a pool physician at Kaiser Permanente Redwood City, California. She lives in the Bay Area with her husband and two sons.

Reiko Johnson MD graduated from the University of Washington Family Medicine Residency in 2006 and has been working in urgent care/occupational medicine. She now lives in New Hampshire with her husband and three daughters and is currently involved with a non-profit to empower girls and women in developing countries.

Although **Crystal Kong-Wong MD** is a 3rd generation San Franciscan, she somehow found herself in the Pacific Northwest. After she graduated from the University of Michigan Medical School, she completed her residency and a chief resident year at the University of Washington. As a Clinical Assistant Professor at the University of Washington in Seattle, she practices full spectrum family medicine including obstetrics, takes care of two kiddos, and works with the Seattle Children's/University of Washington Adult Autism Transition Team. These activities keep her busy, but she still occasionally enjoys her hobbies: cooking ridiculously complicated recipes, golfing, reading, and going to museums. She lives with her husband Brandon, son Micah, and daughter Elise in Seattle.

Heather Kovich MD is a family medicine physician who works for the Indian Health Service on the Navajo Nation in New Mexico. She is mom to two precocious boys and a shaggy black dog. None of them come when she calls. She is constantly grateful for the support of her husband.

Casey Law MD graduated from the University of Iowa Carver College of Medicine where the tradition of medical writing has always been encouraged and celebrated. While there he participated in an elective course on medical writing taught by the talented Margaret LeMay-Lewis and even wrote a poem or two. He now works as a family medicine physician in the Seattle area. Though not writing as much these days as he desires, he still finds recurrent joy in the deep and always enticing waters of the written word. Since residency when his piece was written, his URAC is much better. (see "The Prodigal Son's Brother")

A Latin American Studies major in college, **Kim O'Connor MD** completed medical school and internal medicine residency training and now is an Associate Professor of Medicine at the University of Washington in Seattle. Her time is divided between providing patient care in a primary care setting in Seattle and, as a College Faculty Mentor, teaching clinical skills while mentoring medical students in the School of Medicine at the University of Washington. She is passionate about travel and believes exposure to the world's cultures provides her a unique perspective when working with students and patients. Her academic and teaching interests include patient-provider communication, wellness, and diversity and she embraces opportunities for curriculum development in these areas.

Cynthia Ohata MD wrote her story during her family medicine residency at the University of Washington, where she also completed medical school. As an Assistant Professor, she now enjoys teaching medical students from Rush Medical College and family medicine residents from Advocate Christ Medical Center in Chicago. She endeavors to create thorough, compassionate, and practical primary care. She and her two children are avid martial artists who have achieved black belt status.

Genevieve Pagalilauan MD is the mother of two rambunctious boys and wife to a die-hard University of Michigan fan. She however is a died-in-the-wool University of Washington Husky, having spent undergraduate, medical school, residency, and now as Associate Professor on the faculty at UDub. Currently she works full-time as a general internist, teaching medical students and residents, and mentoring and supporting student efforts in advocacy and community service. In her spare time, which she hopes to have any day now, she enjoys her garden and soccer with her sons.

Hank Pelto MD is an Acting Assistant Professor of Family Medicine in the section of Sports Medicine at the University of Washington. He met the patients in his story during a rich Family Medicine residency at the University of Washington. Whether in primary care or sports medicine he believes deeply in the patient-physician relationship and its ability to enrich the lives of all involved. His professional interests include sports cardiology and the prevention of sudden death in athletes as well as the care of active individuals. Outside of work he enjoys running, golf and spending time with his wife and growing family.

Abigail Plawman MD is motivated to teach students and residents to help develop and refine an understanding of how human beings interact with complex psychosocial situations. She went to medical school at the University of Washington, followed by a Family Medicine residency at Swedish Cherry Hill and finally an Addiction Medicine fellowship at Swedish Ballard, all in Seattle, Washington. She is now on faculty at a new and growing Multi-Care East Pierce Family Medicine Residency Program in Puyallup, Washington and working to develop services for patients who struggle with addiction. Work-life balance still challenges her because she values the importance of relationships both within and outside of medicine. She wrote her contribution as a resident.

Born in the small town of Eatonville, located just outside of Orlando, Florida, **Cherita Raines MD, MPH** had an education journey that guided her around the United States. She started in Atlanta, Georgia for college at Emory University. She completed a post baccalaureate program at Southern Illinois University in Carbondale, Illinois and then made NYC her home for her four years of Mount Sinai School of Medicine. In between her third and fourth year of medical school, she ventured to Boston for a year to get her Master's Degree in Public Health at Harvard School of Public Health. Family Medicine Residency at University of Washington drew her to the Seattle area. The beauty of the Pacific Northwest has kept her there.

She is the Family Medicine Department Chairperson for the Everett Clinic, which has eight satellites. When not seeing patients in her clinic in Marysville, Washington, or at their homes, or delivering their babies, Dr. Raines can be found seeking new outdoor adventures like hiking and skiing. In her spare time she enjoys playing tennis, visiting with friends, and volunteering. Most of all, she loves the personal relationships that she has with her patients; they are the fuel that keeps her going. She considers it an honor to be able to share with you one of the many patient experiences that has left a lasting impression.

Erin Richardson MD wrote her piece during residency in the Department of Family Medicine at the University of Washington. She now practices in a community health center in Seattle where she lives, works, and plays with her husband and family.

A true home-grown Seattleite, **Amy Rodriguez MD** was born on Capital Hill and raised in Ballard, two well known neighborhoods in that city. From an early age, she knew she wanted to do something medical with her life. The path she took to get there was both meandering and interesting, starting with four years as an Army Medic serving in part in South Korea and ending at her current job as a physician at Community Health Center of Snohomish County in Everett, Washington. Amy has a soft spot in her heart for Harborview Medical Center in Seattle where she worked as a receptionist, medical assistant, medical student, resident and an attending physician teaching residents. These days, Amy's favorite haunts are clinic, the Labor and Delivery ward at the hospital, the gym, and her living room couch. She is happiest at a Seattle Thunderbirds hockey game with her kids, knitting, or elbow-deep in amniotic fluid. She is humbled by the trust that her patients put in her and the stories that they tell and she remains constantly excited about her job and the lessons that her patients teach her on a daily basis.

At the time of this note, **Roger A Rosenblatt MD, MPH, MFR** is Professor and Vice Chair of the Department of Family Medicine at the University of Washington School of Medicine, with adjunct academic appointments in Health Services, Global Health, and Forestry. As this somewhat non-standard set of academic affiliations might suggest, he admits to having a short attention span and many interests, from teaching medical students to restoring ancient forests to grappling with the health consequences of climate change. He was the first family medicine resident at the University of Washington, starting in 1971, and the first resident to go to a remote rural clinic during residency as part of the WAMI program in 1972 (Washington, Alaska, Montana, Idaho, now WWAMI which includes Wyoming). He says he had so much fun batting his head against all those insoluble problems that he spent his entire career at the UW, with an exhilarating three year break in the public health service (where he met his wife, Fernne).

Erika Roshanravan MD was born and raised in Switzerland. After meeting her Iranian husband in Chicago, she finished medical school in Switzerland and then moved with him to Seattle for residency. She completed residency in family medicine and then her chief resident year at the University of Washington Family Medicine Residency in 2012. You can find her now taking care of a wide variety of patients, doing full spectrum family medicine, including obstetrics, at Community Health Centers of Snohomish County in Everett, Washington. Working with disadvantaged and uninsured families as her patients, she wonders every day why such a rich country has not yet managed to build a more equitable, sustainable healthcare system. Still interested in resident and medical student education, Erika continues to precept residents at the UW residency clinics on some of her days off. Otherwise she uses that spare time to explore the Northwest with her young son and daughter, husband, and friends, or to travel back home to Switzerland or elsewhere.

Sherilyn Smith MD is a Pediatric Infectious Disease specialist who works at Seattle Children's Hospital. In addition to caring for children with infectious disease related illnesses, she is a Professor of Pediatrics at the University of Washington School of Medicine. In this role, she teaches medical students, residents and fellows about the care of children and their families. Her husband and son support her in all of her endeavors and she cherishes the natural beauty of the Pacific Northwest.

Mick Storck MD arrived to his faculty position at the University of Washington School of Medicine in Seattle via roots in Ohio, North Carolina, and Arizona. He is delighted to be in the chorus of appreciative folks that Dr. Sharon Dobie has gathered with her here to share stories in *Heart Murmurs*. Mick has been a co-learner with his fellow humans beginning in a large family and wandering, in his younger days, down 100,000 miles of road as a hitchhiker, and for the last 30-plus years as a physician on the path with patients, students and colleagues. He served in the USPHS Indian Health Service and for the last 25 years as a pediatric psychiatrist at the long-term state psychiatric hospital for children in Washington State. Mick is ever grateful to be a collaborator alongside all the projects that contribute to our healing ways, sharing life's quandaries, epiphanies, and hopes.

Anthony Suchman, MD, MA, FACP is a practicing internist, health services researcher, consultant at Relationship Centered Health Care, and Professor of Medicine at the University of Rochester, Rochester, New York. He is a leading advocate of Relationship Centered Care. His current work focuses on organizational behavior in healthcare—fostering leadership behavior and work environments that treat staff members in the same way we want them to treat patient and families: relationship centered. He has recently published his second book, *Leading Change in Healthcare* (co-authored with David Sluyter and Penny Williamson), which presents principles and case studies in Relationship-Centered Administration. He and his wife, artist Lynne Feldman, live in Rochester, New York and enjoy hiking in the Finger Lakes.

An attorney in a prior life, **Christina Tanner MD** grew up in Montreal, Quebec, and went to medical school in Halifax, Nova Scotia and enjoys many things—travel, food, literature, languages, skiing, sailing and photography. As a Clinical Associate Professor of Family Medicine, she now practices in Seattle at the University of Washington where she also teaches (and learns from) medical students and residents. She and her husband, Mik, have three globe-trotting daughters.